The Vikings

The Story of a People

by Njord Kane

The Vikings: The Story of a People.

By Njord Kane

Books may be purchased by contacting the publisher and author at: spangenhelm.com

Published on: September 14, 2015 by Spangenhelm Publishing

Interior Design and Cover by: Njord Kane

Library of Congress Control Number: 2015939914

ISBN-13: 978-1-943066-01-8

ISBN-10: 1-943066-01-9

1. Vikings 2. Norse 3. History 4. Europe

Second Edition.

10 9 8 7 6 5 4 3 2

 **Spangenhelm Publishing**
United States

Spangenhelm Publishing is a Read Icon, Inc company

Table of Contents

Preface...i

Chapter 1 - Who were the Vikings?....................................1

Chapter 2 – The Nordic Stone Age.....................................9

Chapter 3 – The Metallic Ages.......................................27

Chapter 4 – The Viking Age..37

Chapter 5 – Norse Religion..95

Chapter 6 – Christianization of the Norse..........................143

Chapter 7 – Norse Language...161

Chapter 8 – Norse Life...173

Chapter 9 – Norse Trade..189

Chapter 10 – Norse Law and Government..............................195

Chapter 11 – Norse Warfare...205

  Norse Battle Tactics 208

Chapter 12 – Norse Armor and Weaponry..............................217

  The Shield...218

  The Ax...224

  The Bow..227

  The Spear..230

  The Atgeir...232

  The Sword..234

  Viking Armor...237

  Viking Helms...241

Chapter 13 – Norse Longships.......................................245

Chapter 14 - The Skræling...251

Chapter 15 - The Jötnar (Giants)..................................261

  References...266

Preface

This book is divided into two parts. The first part tells the Norse story chronologically from an anthropologist's point of view. Starting from the early Norse people during the Stone Age that migrated as hunter-gathers following herds of megafauna, such as Mammoths. From the Stone Age into the gradual progression of settling and forming into a complex society. Detailing the steps of Norse society as they evolved into the far reaching "viking" explorers that changed and modified the World we know today.

The second part of this book highlights specifics about ancient Norse culture, technology, beliefs, and practices.

The Norse were a major indigenous people of Scandinavia and Northern Europe. When we refer to them, we often see the words Vikings and Norse used interchangeably without discrimination. So which term is correct when referring to these people? Do we call them Vikings or Norse?

At first thought, we usually call them Vikings. This is because when we mention the Vikings, immediately everyone knows we're talking about the Norse.

However, the term "Viking" is not actually what the

Norse people called themselves. It was actually something they did.

The word Viking comes from the Old Norse word "víkingr," a term which meant to go raiding and it wasn't always by boat. The word Viking was only later used to refer to the Norse people whom were conducting these raids. There are a variety of other stereotypes commonly associated with "Vikings." Most are simply false stereotypes such as the horned or winged helmet for example.

Calling them "Vikings" is technically incorrect. However it's of such common use today that when we call them Vikings, everyone knows that we're referring to the Norse. Even though Viking was something they did (raid) and not what they were called.. or how they referred to themselves. They were actually called the Norse or Northmen.

A statement of fact is: all Vikings were Norse, but not all Norse were Vikings. In fact, most Norse were farmers – just like everyone else on the planet during the time.

The purpose of this book is to provide a concise and up to date historical chronicle about the Norse people. With so many recent discoveries by archaeologists studying the Norse, there are many things that we had previously thought we knew about the Norse that has changed. This makes the Nordic story as previously taught out of date and in need of being retold. This book tells the Norse story current to today's discoveries, presented in short chapters through each epoch of Nordic history.

We start our story about the Norse from the first proof of existence as an identifiable and distinct people. A people whom migrated into Scandinavia and the Northern European area many thousands of years ago. We then take you through their progression from hunter-gathers into the agricultural settlements that eventually grew into societies.

A journey through the rise and expansion of Nordic culture that forever help form Europe and Western Culture as a whole. Highlighting new discoveries in Norse knowledge and technologies, that were previously a mystery to scientists.

This book is not the single work of the author, but the combined works of hundreds of years by thousands of researchers that have spent lifetimes trying to unravel the story and mystery of the Norse people. There has been so many recent discoveries by modern researchers, the Nordic story has been rewritten from what we thought we used to know about their obscure history. A history that was almost lost in time and obscure mythology.

Part 1

The Beginnings of a People

Chapter 1 - Who were the Vikings?

The "Vikings" were an ancient people that inhabited Northern Europe and Scandinavia known as the Norse (also known as Northmen or Norsemen). The Norse people were spread across Northern Europe, particularly in the regions known today as: Scandinavia (Norway, Sweden, and Finland), Germany, Denmark, Poland, Netherlands, the United Kingdom (England, Scotland, Ireland, and the surrounding islands), Iceland, Russia, Latvia, Lithuania, and Estonia.

These northern people as a whole spoke as their native language, one the various dialects of Norse. The Norse language was a Northern Germanic / Scandinavian language that was in wide use before the Christianization of Northern Europe, Russia, and Scandinavia.

The Norse are today most commonly known to people as the "Vikings." However, the term "viking" was not actually what the Norse people called themselves. It was something that they did. The word "viking" comes from the Old Norse word "víkingr," a term which meant to go raiding for loot and it was something that wasn't always done by boat. A Viking was a Norse Raider.

The word viking was only later misused when referring to the Norse people as a whole, instead of just those specific Norsemen whom conducted the Viking raids. Simply put, a "Viking" is a raider, or more correctly; a Norseman whom went raiding. In more precise terms, a Viking is a Norse Raider.

With this in mind, we know that calling the Norse people "Vikings" as a whole is incorrect. However it is of such common use today that when someone calls them Vikings, everyone knows that they are talking about the Norse. Although, in most cases, they are referring to Norse Raiders, in which case, "Vikings" would be correct. But to reiterate, viking was something they did (raid) and the people were actually called the Norse.

A statement of fact is: **all Vikings were Norse, but not all Norse were Vikings**.

In fact, most Norse were farmers and tradesman – just like everyone else on the planet. I had said all of this in the preface of this book, but found it necessary to repeat myself because I simply can't stress this fact enough.

There are also many other misunderstandings and stereotypes that are commonly associated with the term "Viking." One of the most common false stereotypes about the Norse and especially of viking raiders is that of the horned or winged helmet for example.

The Norse never wore winged or horned helmets - that is fiction. The types of helmets the Norse wore is discussed further ahead in this book's chapter about *Norse Arms and Armor*.

The winged and horned helmet were mistakenly used to depict Vikings in an opera. The opera singer's costumes of winged and horned helmets stuck as a common belief as to what the Norse used to look like and what they wore.

Statue of a Viking in Gimli, Manitoba (Canada).[42]

As glorious as many of these false depictions may be; such as horned helmets being a sort of universal icon as to identify Vikings.

We'll clear up these misconceptions as we go further along in the book and look closely at what the Norse really did and what they were really like. We'll look at the facts of what was real about the Norse people and their culture. We'll also look specifically at the Norse that infamously raided during the Viking Era, giving them the label as Vikings.

The history of the Norse people goes all the way back to the Stone Age, but they are best known for a period of time when they raided several parts of Europe known as the Viking Age.

The Viking Age is typically recorded in history as occurring approximately around 793 AD to 1066 AD. This period of time is not the time span of the Norse people themselves, nor was it the peak of their civilization. This is merely the height of the time when the Norse people were mostly written about. The time when they reached out and went out on viking adventures. A time when the World noticed them and were fearful.

The Viking Age began somewhere just before the date of 800 AD. The actual beginning of the Viking Age is a bit foggy and different locations argue different time periods of when viking raids actually began to occur.

To abolish this argument, it is generally accepted in the academic community that the official beginning of the Viking Age is to have begun on the 8th of June 793 AD. This date is when there is a formal recording made of when Norse Raiders (Vikings) made an attack on the monastery at Lindisfarne, an island off the northeast coast of England.

The attack came unexpected, as it was an unguarded religious community of Christian monks. An easy target for Vikings sailing around the coast in search of a place

4

they can easily raid and loot.

The Viking raiders were seeking an easy target that was close to the water, so they didn't have to go far from their boats. The Norse preferred to raid near their boats to allow them a hasty escape before reinforcements could come.

Allowing the Vikings to surprise attack, loot, and vacate before anyone really knew what happened.

Lindisfarne Priory Viking stone, a 9th Century grave marker. [41]

Lindisfarne was a defenseless place known as the "Holy Island." The viking raid on it caused much consternation throughout the Christian World and is most often marked as being the "official" beginning of the Viking Age.

This map shows the location of the Holy Island, Lindisfarne on the northeastern coast of Northumbria of the modern day UK Island. The raiding Norse had probably landed near the location from the sea and sailed up or down the coast until they spotted a location to attack.

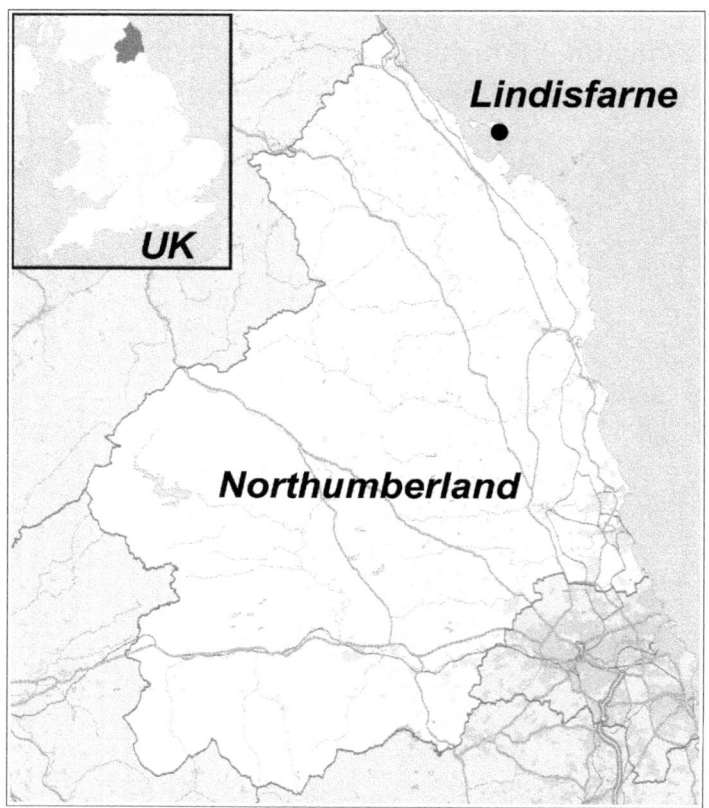

Holy Island of Lindisfarne shown within Northumberland, UK.[43]

The Viking Age is the period of time when the Norse are most often talked about. The Age when the Norse invaded much of Europe during a time when they became known as the Vikings.

The Viking Age is not the beginning of the Norse people

or the start of their culture. The roots of the Norse go back even further. All the way back to the Megalithic and Neolithic Eras of the Stone Age.

The Stone age for the Norse was very different than what we were taught about the Stone Age in regards to other cultures. Other cultures such as the Mediterranean Cultures are where we gathered most of our information about the stone ages, the bronze age, and the iron ages of humankind in general. But the Norse people experienced the change of the Ages much differently than other cultures.

The Stone Ages, the Bronze (Copper) Age, and the Iron ages for the Norse progressed very different that that of the rest of the World. So different were the early stages of Nordic cultural evolution that they have their own separate categories and classifications for their cultural evolutionary eras. The culturally specific Norse classifications are labeled as: *The Nordic Stone Age, The Nordic Bronze Age*, and *the Nordic Iron Age*. The Nordic Iron Age is broken down into its own separate stages as well.

The Norse made the best of what they had available to them and with their unique regional situation, adapted with an uncanny sense of innovativeness. Their ability to trade and reach areas of trading to better improve their way of life was unmatched by any other culture in their day.

Nordic innovative technology that is still unmatched today. Their willingness to reach out far to other populations and cultures made them one of the most influential cultures out there.

Chapter 2 – The Nordic Stone Age

From around the time during the Lower Paleolithic Era, which was about 1.8 million years ago, into the Upper Paleolithic Era, or 20,000 years ago; Europe was sparsely populated by Homo Erectus and Homo Neanderthalensis. These were the ancient ancestors of modern humans. They were a hunter-gather type of people whom were eventually replaced by Homo Sapiens, modern humans.

Survival was hard and basic survival techniques were limited in an ever changing and unpredictable climate. The general practice of survival was to hunt and find whatever it was that they could scavenge to eat in order to survive. Hunting megafauna (large animals) was one of the most practiced means by groups that were able to survive in this environment.

To hunt these large animals, they had to develop ways to take them down. This included designing specialized tools such as spears and javelins to hunt. Archeologists have found 380,000 year old wooden javelins belonging to these hunters in the Nordic Stone Age area. These javelins are the oldest complete hunting weapons ever found anywhere in the world and they were discovered in Schoningen, Germany.[1]

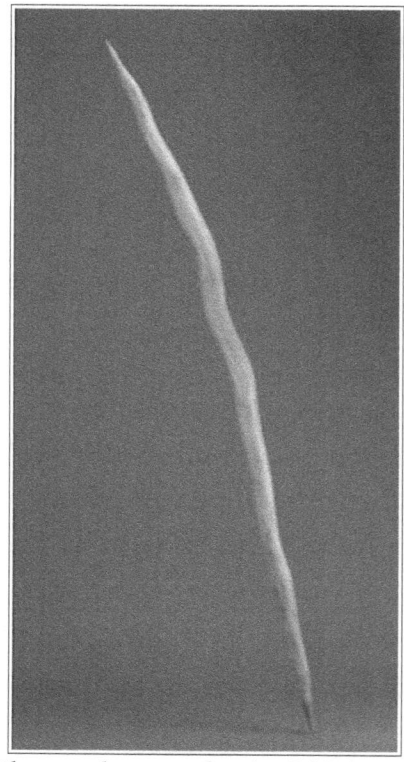

One of three wooden spears found at Schöningen, Germany.[44]

During the Upper Paleolithic to the Mesolithic Era, ranging from about 43,000 to 6,000 years ago, Europe's homo sapiens (human) hunter-gatherer populations gradually began to increase in number. During the last glacial maximum (Ice Age), much of Europe was depopulated because of the changed climate. After the thaw, Europe was then re-settled again approximately 15,000 years ago.

During this period of repopulation, groups of Europeans migrated long distances following the edge of the glacial ice in search of food. They were mostly hunting seals and following them along the edge of the ice and the sea. Some groups that were following seals and other marine food stuffs had made it all the way to North America traveling along the ice's edge that bridged across from Europe to North America.

We know that Stone Age Europeans had crossed over into North America during this time because several dozen European-style stone tools, dating back between 19,000 and 26,000 years, have been discovered at six different locations along the U. S. East Coast. What's more, chemical analysis carried out on a 19,000 year old stone knife found in Virginia, USA revealed that it was made of a French-originating flint.

That's a long distance for Stone Age people to travel, but it was necessary for their survival. They followed the food they were hunting in order to survive the exceptionally harsh climate.

What became of the Stone Aged Paleo-Europeans that had migrated to North America is still a puzzle for researchers to unravel. It is unclear as to whether or not they completely died out or if they attempted any form of settling. The most probable conclusion is that they continued to wander, hunting and searching for food until they eventually died out.

We do know Paleo-Europeans began entering the previously uninhabited North America at about the same time as the Paleo-Indians began crossing over via the Bering Sea land-bridge (Beringia). Similarly, Paleo-Indians followed game across the land-ice bridge much the same way as the Paleo-Europeans did on the opposite side of the continent.

As the glacial ice receded and the climate warmed up, the fauna that these stone aged hunter-gatherers hunted changed as some of the large herd animals began to become more scarce. There were fewer mammoth herds as the number of these animals began to dwindle.

Fortunately, the warmer climate brought new sources of meat, such as growing herds of reindeer, that had become more readily available over time. Eventually, reindeer became a main source of hide, bone, antler, and of course a primary source of meat.

It was during this time of the Nordic Stone Age that the Norse people existed as nomadic reindeer hunters. From 13,500 BC to 11,000 BC is a period of time during the Nordic Stone Age that is called the **Hamburg Culture.** This time period is classified by the shouldered spear and arrow points discovered that date to the period and zinken tools found that the Hamburg Culture people used as chisels when working with horns.

Also specific to the Hamburg Culture are the tanged Havelte-type arrow head points found which are described as being unique to the Hamburg Culture exclusively.

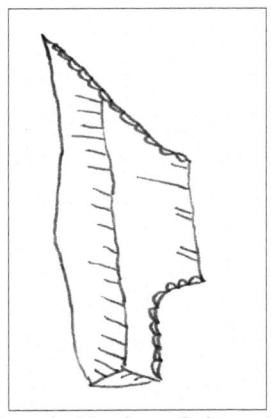

An illustration of a Hamburg Culture Arrow Head.[2]

Rock circles were also found in small settlements that are attributed to being used as weights to hold down the coverings of teepees. A teepee (also tepee and tipi) is a conical tent usually made of animal skins and supported by wooden poles. Teepees were used by primitive Nordic people just like the Great Plains Indians of North America and Saami people North of them in Scandinavia.

Within these sites were a great amount of reindeer horn and bone remnants which shows that the reindeer were a very important prey. It appears that they lived in small groups that ranged from East of Poland to Northern France and Southern Scandinavia. It has also been discovered that they migrated along the Norwegian coast during the summer months because the sea level at the time was about 50 meters lower than it is today.

After this period in the late upper paleolithic age at around 11000 BC to 10000 BC came the **Ahrensburg Culture** with the complete extinction of megafauna, such as the mammoth. The ice began to recede in lower Sweden and Denmark from the Younger Dryas event (The Big Freeze) which caused much deforestation and there were land stretches exposed which are now under the North and Baltic Seas. This allowed these migrating hunter groups to reach areas by foot that later could only be reached by boats.

These Nordic nomads continued to hunt grazing wild reindeer and now had more incentive to exploit marine resources that became more accessible.

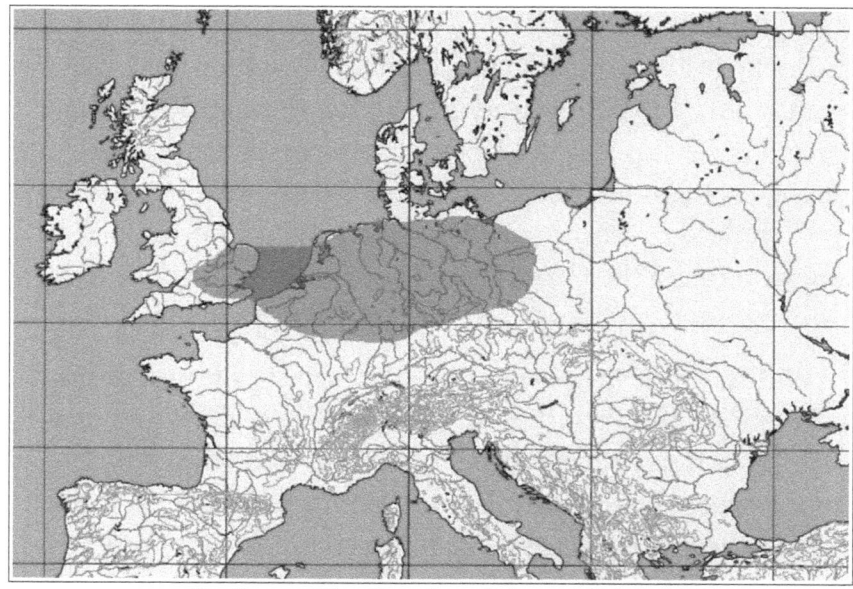

The Range of the Ahrensburg Culture. (Albin L. 2009)

The arrowheads of this time period changed to a shouldered, tanged point. This was a marked improvement in hunting methods as better tools were being made. With improved weapons and tools, hunters were able to hunt more proficiently and expand the variety of prey they hunted.

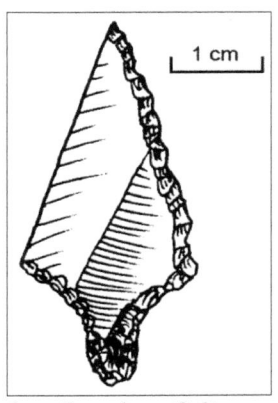

Drawing of an Ahrensburg Culture arrow head.[3]

Fish hooks have also been discovered, showing an improvement from relying on spear fishing by having the ability and knowledge to angle for fish. This may have contributed to a slowing in culture development, because the Neolithic Age (New Stone Age) is estimated to have begun around 5,000 BC in Northern Europe. This is about 4000 years after the Neolithic Age had already began in Southern Europe.

The **Linear Pottery culture** (Linearbandkeramik) was the next major archaeological horizon of the Northern European Neolithic Age happening at around 5500 BC to 4500 BC. This culture migrated less and began the gradual process of more permanently settling in areas. It was during the Linear Pottery culture that a trait started to co-evolve with the culture of dairy farming.

A significant change in lifestyle when agriculture began to develop with the keeping of livestock in lieu of complete dependency of hunting and gathering for survival. This was also a time where the transition from living a nomadic lifestyle in teepees to remaining in one place and living in more permanent structures such as communal long houses.

Excavations have revealed a large fortified settlement at Oslonki, Poland which dates to around 4300 BC that had nearly thirty trapezoidal longhouses located within in. The rectangular longhouses were between seven and forty-five meters long and were between five and seven meters wide. They were built with massive timber posts chinked with wattle and daub mortar.

Within them, and the nearly eighty grave sites on location, simple pottery items were found consisting of simple cups, bowls, vases, and jugs without handles. These pottery items were obviously designed as kitchen dishes and for transport and trade of food and liquids.

Linear Band Pottery.[4]

The use and life style associated with the Linear Band Pottery Culture began somewhat inland nearer other cultures and was most probably a learned concept from neighboring peoples to the South and East. The culture did not spread North or near the coastlines until later.

The culture that developed simultaneously to the North of the Linear Band Culture was the **Ertebølle culture.** This culture existed predominately in the Southern Areas of Scandinavia from about 5300 BC to 3950 BC.

These people were hunter-gatherers that also relied on fishing and had some pottery making within their culture as well. This was about the time that this culture had some sparse transition to animal husbandry, such as cows and pigs. They didn't practice cultivation yet, but they did trade for barley and emmer wheat (also known as farro or hulled wheat) from tribes south of them and engaged in seasonal cultivation of wild crops.

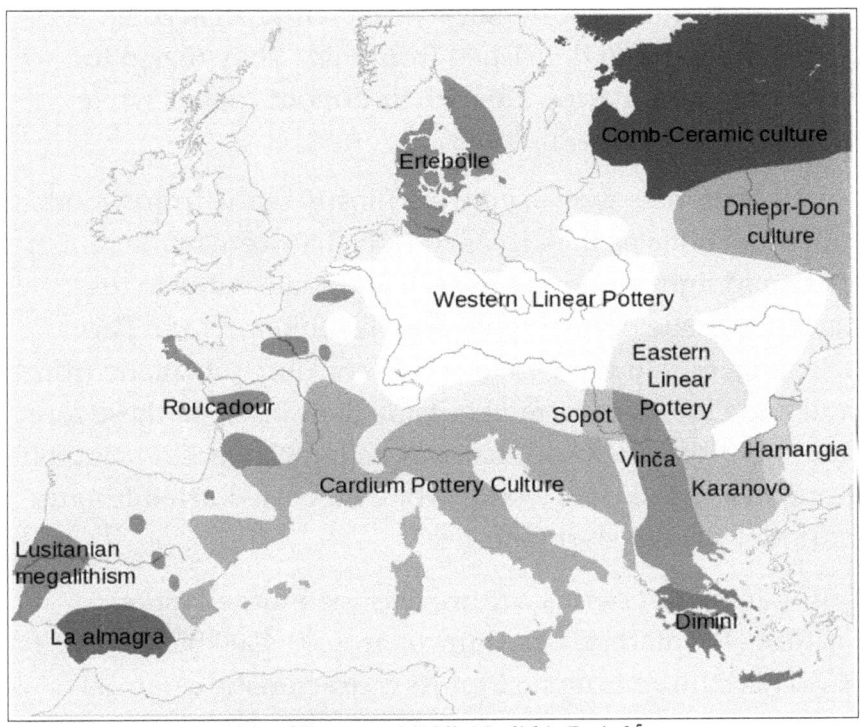

Map of European Middle Neolithic Period.[5]

By looking at the map above, you can see the proximity of the Western Linear Pottery cultures and the Ertebølle Cultures which encompass the majority of the Early Norse inhabited areas. This explains the trade exchanges and similarities between the cultures at that time. Their proximity and regular interaction with each other allowed exchanges in technology and ideas.

The climate became warmer than it is today in those regions and the water level soon became significantly higher. It was about five to six meters higher on the Baltic coastline than it is Today. Jutland (Denmark) was an archipelago during this time of small island chains and groups. The inland waters were rich with fish and the people living there flourished from this. They fished for these abundant marine life in their dugout canoes while also hunting whales and seals.

The materials they used were mostly made from wood, antler and bone as they lived in huts that were made of brush and light wood that was in abundance due to the warmer climate occurring during this time period. This was along with having milder winters. Fire pits made from mud and clay were formed outside their huts. In these fore pits, they used firewood that was usually collected from the shorelines (dried drift wood) while they used dried fungus for tinder to help start their fires.

Evolving out of this culture was the **Funnelbeaker Culture** (Trichterbecherkultur) of around 4300 BC to 2800 BC. This culture is named for its characteristic ceramics with funnel-shaped tops which were probably used for drinking.

The people of this culture lived more inland in settlements that were located near those of the previous Ertebølle culture on the coast. They lived in single-family waffle and daub houses that were made from weaved lattice strips of wood or sticks and then 'daubed' with sticky material generally made from mud, clay, and straw mixtures.

The livelihood of these people relied on farming and animal husbandry which became their major sources of food. They raised sheep, cattle, pigs, and goats but also continued to rely on some hunting and fishing for food stuffs. They grew primitive wheat and barley on small patches, but these resources were fast depleted and still had not developed into a major dietary staple yet.

There was some small scale mining and collection of flint stone, which was traded into areas that lacked flint stone, such as the Scandinavian hinterlands. This culture also traded and imported copper items from Central Europe, especially tools, daggers, and axes.

During this time period a communal pile dwellings, also called stilt houses, were built and improved over several years by some communities that were only inhabited during the summer months. These buildings were used as social centers where clans gathered for festivities after the summer's hunting and harvesting season.

This may also have been an early concept of the Norse "Thing," where free men from different clans met to trade and negotiate disputes and make agreements. There were usually about 100 hearths made of limestone that were evenly distributed across the pile dwelling in huts that were supported by the many hazel stilts.

Around these limestone hearths, researchers found an abundance of residue from meals of charred wheat and barley, split and charred crab apples, hazel nut shells, and bone from cattle, sheep and pigs. There were also remains from game such as red deer, moose, wolf, and bear. Additionally, researchers found remains from fowl such as mallard and black grouse and the remains of fish such as northern pike and perch. This shows how expanded their diets were becoming and the variety of meat consumed that they fished and hunted for.

The ceramics of these people were the same as those of the hunter-gatherer Pitted Ware culture, but the tools and weapons were the same as those of the Funnelbeaker culture. This shows a mixture of culture and technology shared between them.

The remains of craftsmanship were relatively few, suggesting that their tools were transported to the communal pile dwellings from the workshops where they lived the majority of the time. Meaning, they only came to the communal sites for short periods of time to trade and exchange ideas. Additionally meeting for religious rites and probably to make sacrifices to their gods.

Among the most remarkable finds in these communal sites were double edged battle axes, which appear to have played an important role in their culture as far as being symbols of status.

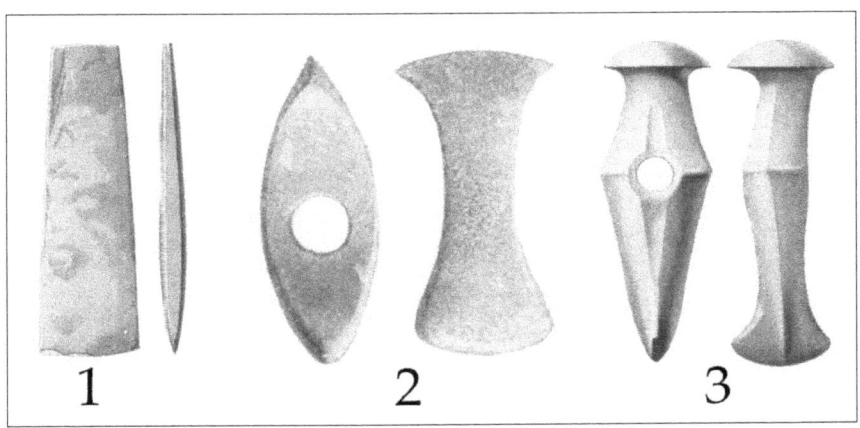

Axes from the Funnelbeaker culture. 1. thin-neck ax, 2. double-edged battle ax, 3. polygonal battle ax.[6]

During the time of these Nordic Stone Age cultures, a prevalence of a gene that allowed adults of Northern European descent to digest lactose originated and spread to other cultures to become virtually universal. This was a genetic variant that was either rare or completely absent in early farmers from Central Europe.

Lactase is an enzyme produced in the digestive system of infants and some (mostly European) adult humans to break down lactose. The lactase enzyme is essential in the digestion of whole milk. The absence of the lactase enzyme is what causes a person consuming dairy products to experience the symptoms of lactose intolerance. Ancient DNA extracted from three individuals belonging to the Funnelbeaker Culture in Gökhem, Sweden were found to possess these traits.

This genetic trait made cattle an even more important resource to the Norse than just that of meat and hide. The milk could now be regularly harvested for consumption, which later evolved into cheese, butter and other dairy products which became a very important part of their culture.

Evolving from this culture followed the **Battleaxe Culture**, also known as the **Boat-Ax Culture** or more accurately, the **Corded Ware Culture** of approximately 2800 BC that continued well into the Nordic Bronze Age that began around 1700 BC. The name 'boat-ax' comes from the fact that the over 3000 battle axes found scattered throughout the Nordic areas of Scandinavia made from ground stone were shaped similar to that of boats.

Boat-shaped battle axes typical of the Battle Ax Culture.[7]

This time period has also been nicknamed the Age of Crushed Skulls by Swedish writer Herman Lindqvist. due to evidence of skull damage in grave sites caused by axes. This is also highly suggestive as to why the style of spangenhelm helmets worn by the Norse may have evolved to the distinctive conical shape as a means to protect the head from such blows.

The culture of this age gets its more accurate label as the Corded-Ware Culture, because of the change in pottery during this time period. Pottery that was highly influenced from pastoral societies on the Central European steppes.

Corded-Ware pottery from around 2500 BC.[8]

The span of Corded-Ware Culture coincides with the Funnel-Beaker Culture as improvements were learned from neighboring groups and a greater reliance on farming began to evolve. Much of the early distribution of this culture was more inland in its beginnings than from the coastal regions. The people of this culture shared many features of the Funnel-Beaker Culture such as use of horses and wheeled carts (which were possibly drawn by oxen) that originated from the European steppes.

The improvements from this culture spread quickly to other settlements due to the aforementioned higher sea levels which instead of being a hindrance and dividing the cultures, allowed them to use the dividing waterways and the seas as highways. This developed into a maritime culture that enhanced their geographical spread and economies with expanded trade.

Chapter 3 – The Metallic Ages

The Norse "Metallic Ages," so called because they date the time periods when the Norse people are recorded to have been working with metals such as: copper, bronze, and iron. This Age also includes the Migration Period (the Age of Heroes), because it happened during the time of the Germanic Iron Age when there were great southerly migrations of the Nordic people.

The Norse Metallic Ages are:

- The Nordic Bronze Age 1700 BC –500 BC.

- The Pre-Roman Iron Age 500 BC – 1 AD.

- The Roman Iron Age 1 AD - 400 AD.

- The Germanic Iron Age 400 AD – 800 AD.

- The Migration Period ("The Heroic Age") 400 - 800 AD.

The **Nordic Bronze Age**, also called the Northern Bronze Age, occurred approximately 1700 BC through 500 BC. The Scandinavian Norse joined the European Bronze

Age relatively late and began from importing goods such as European bronze and gold items by means of trade.

During this time many rock carvings depicting ships began showing up, along with the early burial custom of making monument "Stone Ship" burial mounds. These Stone Ships varied in size from small to huge and were generally around other burial grounds and religious ceremonial locations. It is believed that the building of these ships, along with equipping the bereaved with other items, would help them along in their journey to underworld of Hel.

Two Stone Ships (Burial Grounds).[9]

There wasn't a written language developed during this Age yet and most stone carvings depicted either ships or elk. The stones are dated in comparison with bronze axes and swords found from the same era.

Also marking the Nordic Bronze Age was the fact that there was a warmer climate in the region similar to that of Northern France today due to climate change that happened around 2700 BC. This allowed Norse communities to live closer together in denser populations as they experienced better farming conditions. Grapes were even grown in parts of Scandinavia during this time.

This did change because during the end of the Norse Bronze Age, from around 850 BC through 650 BC, the climate changed again becoming colder and wetter which dramatically altered living conditions and southerly migrations began.

The Norse then developed into what's called the **Pre-Roman Iron Age** that ranged from around 500 BC through until the 1st century BC when they came into contact with the Romans. This time line is the earliest part of the Nordic Iron Age that occurred in Norse inhabited areas where a wealth of archaeological artifacts have surfaced leading scholars to believe that Pre-Roman Iron Age Norse evolved without completely making a transition out of the Nordic Bronze age.

Although the use of iron began to increase, bronze was still mostly used during this time. The Norse use of iron gradually increased with strong Celtic influences until greater contact with the Romans in the 1st century BC, when

Nordic use of Iron became even more influenced by Roman culture.

It was during this period of the Nordic Pre-Iron age before 71 BC, that many Norse came down to unite with a Germanic leader by the name of Ariovistus. Ariovistus had promised the Norse lands for resettlement in Gallic areas as reward for joining his army and fighting for him.

Ariovistus is described by Julius Caesar's firsthand account of the Gallic Wars, as rex Germanorum (King of Germania), even though Germania wasn't united under a single King. The Celtic/Gallic Sequani People asked Ariovistus for assistance in their war against their hereditary rivals, the Gallic Aedui. The Aedui people were aligned with the Romans and the Sequani were in need of assistance in their war against them. Ariovistus seen this as an opportunity for expansion.

Ariovistus, with an army built up from various Germanic and Norse tribes, came to the assistance of the Sequani and defeated the Aedui. However, the Sequani people ended up worse off then before and had lost a third of their lands that were seized by Ariovistus, whom threatened to take a third more because he had to make room and provide the promised settlements for the approximate 24,000 Norse Harudes that had come to assist him from the North. He had also subjugated the Sequani people he had come to help into semi slavery.

The Harudes (or Charudes) were the Norse/Germanic group first mentioned by Julius Caesar as one of the tribes whom had joined Ariovistus crossing the Rhine River to battle the Gallic Aedui. The Norse Harudes had gathered in Jutland (Denmark Today) from the North in Scandinavia and then came South to join with the Germanic tribes that were forming. Their name suggests that they may have come from Hardanger region in the county of Hordaland, Norway and sailed to Jutland.

The Sequani, whom had asked Ariovistus for help but became subjugated and lost their lands in doing so, appealed to their previous enemies the Romans for help now. Julius Caesar came to their aid and drove back the Germanic and Norse tribesmen across the Rhine in 58 BC. However afterward, various tribesmen continued opportunistic raids on Gaul. They would cross the Rhine to raid and then afterwards sought refuge from retaliation by crossing back to the eastern side of the Rhine. This pushed Caesar to build a bridge to cross the Rhine and confront the opportunistic raiders and to show support for the Germanic tribe, the Ubians that were also allied with the Romans.

The first bridge Caesar had built in 58 BC, was built with a Legion of 40,000 troops in ten days. He crossed his army into Germania and burnt down some villages, but the tribes had moved eastward and converged together to meet Caesar's army in force. Caesar had heard of this plan and crossed back over the Rhine into Gaul and took the bridge down with him. He had only been in the area for 18 days.

In 55 BC, Caesar came again with his army and built a new bridge within a few days and again crossed the Rhine. However, the tribes retreated so Caesar returned back into Gaul and took his second bridge down as he did so. Caesar had displayed to the Norse and Germanic tribes that the Rhine wasn't a natural obstacle that would provide them with security from the Romans, as Rome could cross the river at any time they wished. This act secured the eastern front of Gaul, which later had built permanent bridges for trade with allied Germanic tribes that sought out the stability that Rome offered.

This was during the time period known in the Nordic Iron Ages as the **Roman Iron Age**, which ran from around 1 BC to 400 AD, when the Roman Empire had the greatest hold and influence over the Germanic tribes to the north of their empire. An Roman influence that reached all the way into Scandinavia, as climate change continued to push many Norse south to seek places for resettlement.

This was also a time when a great amount of imported goods spread throughout Scandinavia that originated from the Roman Empire such as coins, glass beakers, bronze and iron items such as weapons and other objects. More gold and silver came into Nordic regions towards the end of the Roman Iron Age when Rome began to falter and were ransacked more often by neighboring Germanic tribes.

At the end of the Roman Iron Age, cultural change began happening in Norse areas that was again also influenced by climatic changes that had caused dramatic changes in the flora and fauna. This period in Scandinavia is called the **"Findless Age"** due to the lack of archaeological finds resulting from the scarcity of populations in the area that left behind few traces of their presence. The deteriorating climate pushed Norse populations south as they sought better more arable lands.

This "findless" time period is called the **Migration Age** which happened at the same time as the **Germanic Iron Age** that occurred from 400 AD to 800 AD. It is a time period that is also called the "Heroic Age" and the period of "Barbarian Invasions," because of the consequence of Norse southerly migrations that encroached into the lands of other tribes that were already present. This Nordic incursion caused much friction between pre-existing populations and resulted in many battles and wars. The result of some of these many battles became Sagas about warrior heroes – making it the Heroic Age.

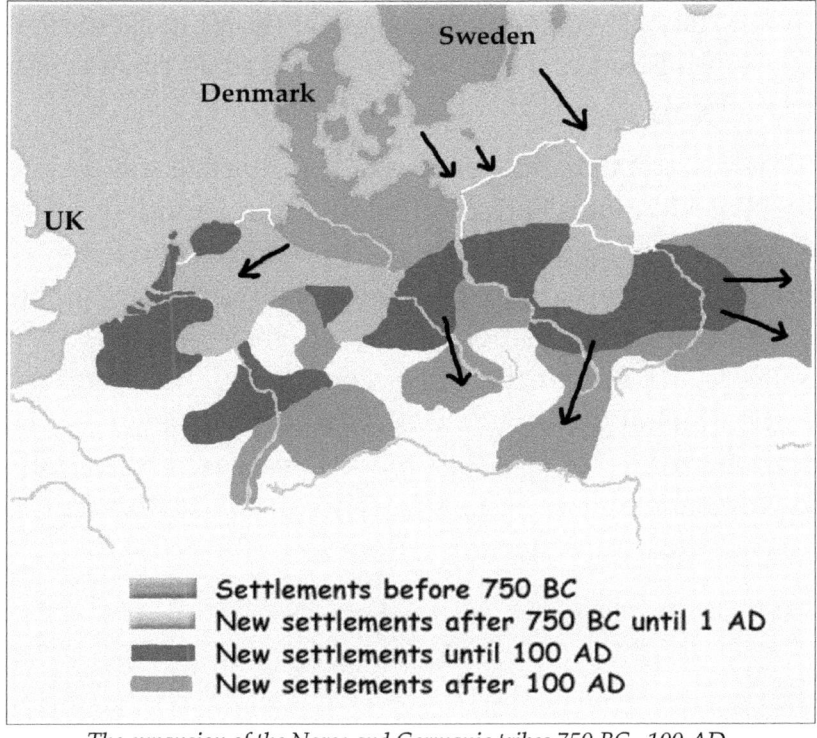

The expansion of the Norse and Germanic tribes 750 BC– 100 AD.

The waning of the once powerful Roman Empire and the growing Celtic and Germanic Kingdoms led to an increase in gold flowing in the north resulting in many works of gold as the Norse used it to make decorative ornaments. After Rome fell, gold then became scarce in the northern regions and the Norse began to use gilded bronze once again.

The Nordic Migration Period happened in two phases. The first phase happening between 300 AD to 500 AD, which put control of the then Western Roman Empire into the hands of the Germanic people.

The second phase of migrations took place 500 AD through 700 AD with settlements expanding into Central and Eastern Europe. This expansion spread all the way into the Lombardy region of Northern Italy.

There is some dispute as to whether this age should be called the Migration Period or the Invasion Period. As there are several explanations as to why the sudden and heavy appearance of 'barbarians' on the Roman frontiers. Climate change pushing populations south into more fertile croplands and the effect of tribes coming in from every direction pushing one people into another, causing a 'domino-effect.' It's also seen that the increased barbarian and Norse movements into formerly controlled Roman lands are the result of a falling Rome, not the cause.

Chapter 4 – The Viking Age

In most cases, the Norse "Viking Age" is recorded to have officially began in 793 AD with the first recorded raid on an undefended monastery through to 1066 AD, ending with the Battle of Hastings. However, these dates vary upon scholars. The Battle of Hastings wasn't exactly the end of the Viking Age, because the Norse were spread out across Europe and Viking raids continued to take place in other locations.

With that said, dating the conclusion of the Viking Age is fairly generic because Viking raids were sporadic in many locations and when one area was under control, another area was being raided. Additionally, this was because Viking raiders weren't unified efforts and most Norsemen tended to 'vikingr' (raid) at their own whim.

This places the conclusion of the Viking Age at approximately the beginning of the 12th Century-ish. This is also about the time when Norse and other Kingdoms were becoming increasingly solidified and more able to repel Viking incursions. This was also around the time when the

Christianization of Northern Europe and Norse dominated lands began to take a firmer hold. So dating the exact end of the Viking Age is vague at best.

The same can be said about the approximate beginning of the Viking Age as well. Although it's officially marked by most scholars as beginning in 793 AD with the raid on the Lindisfarne Monastery, it wasn't a new concept for the Norse to go "vikingr' (raid). Viking raids were already occurring in a vast range of other areas, including France.

Nevertheless the most accepted official start of the Viking Age is recorded to have begun on June 8th, 793 AD when Norse raiders landed on the island of Lindisfarne and attacked the Christian Monastery located there, killing the monks and seizing the valuables.

Viking raids by opportunistic Norsemen also began occurring in frequency at other locations, such as the island of Iona in Scotland in 794 AD. By 795 AD, Christian Monasteries along Ireland's coast were being raided regularly by small Viking groups for the first 40 years. After that, large Viking fleets began showing up.

Viking Raids had begun with regularity on the western coast of Francia (France) in 790 to 800 AD. Normandy, where they had been raiding, actually takes its name from the Viking raiders whom they called Normanii (Norsemen or Men of the North). The Norse raiders seized upon internal turmoil within the leadership of France, so they invaded and seized the region, which later became known as Normandy.

So Viking raids were already occurring in many

locations at the time. What made the Lindisfarne significant to mark it as the official beginning of the Viking Age was because it was the earliest official recording of a Viking raid.

The raid had caused much stir in the Christian world because the Norsemen attacked an unarmed religious compound and killed all the monks that inhabited it. At the time, it was naturally assumed that a religious compound such as a Christian monastery was safe from any kind of attack. The Norse dissolved this illusion.

Although the Viking raids were sporadic, they were very violent when they occurred. The speed and violence of these raids happened without warning and spread much fear to everyone that heard about them. These speedy violent attacks from coastlines and rivers marked the beginning of the **Viking Age of Invasion** by means of the Longship.

Viking Ship, Pre-800 AD.[46]

What helped the Viking raiders during this time period was the fact that England was relaxed with its isolated communities along the edges of coasts, islands, peninsulas, and other waterway inlets. These communities were completely unguarded without a second thought to any dangers from the sea.

This complacency opened the door to Norse raiders as being easy pickings. There was simply an abundance of unguarded and unarmed settlements located near the water that were ripe for Viking raids that were easily reachable by longboat. This allowed the Norse raiders to arrive conveniently by longboat, quickly raid the settlement, and then leave with their plunder uncontested.

Sporadic small scale Viking raids continued across the northern and eastern coastal shores of England, Scotland, and Ireland. The extensive raids in Ireland eventually led to settlements and the founding of Limerick in 812 AD.

At this time, a Norwegian Viking by the name of "Naddodd" became one of the first settlers of the Faroe Islands. He's also credited for discovering Iceland when he was sailing from Norway to the Faroe Islands and got lost. After briefly exploring the Island looking for inhabitants, he returned to his boat and it started snowing, so he named the place Snæland (Snowland), which later became called Ísland (Iceland).

As time passed and word got around about the easy picking of the Islands, the number of raiders grew in size. In 832 AD, a large Viking fleet of about 120 ships had invaded kingdoms in Ireland's eastern and northern coasts. More Norse settlements began to form and the Norse presence started growing even larger in the region.

The Danes came upon the Isle of Sheppey in 835 AD, which is just off the northern coast of Kent, England. After successfully raiding the Isle, they began moving northward looking for more places to raid. Raids by various Norsemen started becoming a regular occurrence to the inhabitants of England, Scotland, and Ireland.

Three years later, in 838 AD, a small Viking party entered the River Liffey and established a base called a "Longphort." This base eventually became the city of Dublin. The Vikings also established other longphorts in locations now called Cork, Limerick, Waterford, and Wexford. The Vikings could sail through on the main rivers and branch off into different areas of the country.

In Scotland, the highly navigable Rivers Tay and Earn were entered by a large Viking fleet in 839 AD. The Norse invaders were able to reach into the very heart of the Pictish kingdom of Fortriu. The Norse defeated the King of the Picts, Eogán mac Óengusa, his brother Bran and the King of the Scots of Dál Riata, Áed mac Boanta, along with many other members of the Pictish aristocracy which were all killed in battle against the invaders.

Depiction of a Pict Warrior.[45]

The Norse, rather than their usual summer raids sailing from Scandinavia or the mainland, waited in Ireland where they had established several strategic bases and then raided parts of England during the winter between 840 AD and 841 AD. Whereas when inhabitants were already worried about the Vikings attacking in the Summer months, now had to now worry about the Winters too.

It was during this time, which was during the reign of Louis the Pious, the King of the Franks, the Vikings were also carrying out raids on Frankish areas primarily in the summer and then wintering in Scandinavia. It wasn't long until several coastal areas had become lost to the Norse invaders as Vikings took advantage of the quarrels within the Frankish royal family caused after the death of Louis the Pious.

The royal family's quarrels caused so much instability in the Frankish region that the Norse seized the opportunity to settle their first colony in the southwest (Gascony) of the Kingdom of Francia. This area had been more or less abandoned by the Frankish kings after their two defeats at Roncevaux Pass on the Spanish border.

The incursions on the River Seine in Francia in 841 AD had caused severe damage to Rouen and Jumièges. The Vikings attacking these Francia regions sought to capture the treasures stored at monasteries, which were easy prey given that the monks lacked any defensive capability.

The Vikings had set up a permanent base in the mouth of the Loire River in 842 AD where they could now strike at places as far as Northern Spain, such as Cadiz which was attacked in 844 AD. In some of their raids on Spain, the Vikings were crushed either by the Kingdom of Asturias or the Emirate armies. The Vikings that did settled in these areas in Spain, such as in Al-Andalus, had eventually become "Hispanized," but kept their ethnic identity and culture.

In 844 AD, many dozens of Dragon Ships (Drakkars)

appeared in the mouth of the Tagus river, along the border of Portugal and Spain. After a siege, the Vikings successfully conquered Lisbon (Al-Ushbuna). The Norse invaders left after 13 days, following a resistance led by Alah Ibn Hazm and the city's inhabitants. Another raid on Lisbon was attempted by the Norse in 966 AD, but was without any success.

Viking raids ruthlessly continued on the divided kingdoms of Francia (the Kingdoms of the Franks, Modern France). The infamous **Ragnar Lothbrok** with 120 ships and 5000 warriors landed in Francia near the mouth of the Seine River and began ravaging Western Francia. During these attacks, the city of Rouen had fallen to the Norse invaders.

Then Carolivenna fell victim and was attacked next in the Viking's search for silver and other valuables. Even the city of Paris fell and King Charles "the Bald" was forced to pay Ragnar a large bribery of silver not to sack it in 845 AD.

However, opportunistic Vikings still regularly patrolled the rivers and waterways of West Francia after discovering the easy pickings of the rich churches and monasteries.

Legend has it that many of the raids conducted on England, Francia and Frisia during this time were led by Ragnar Lothbrok. **Ragnar Lothbrok** (also Ragnar Lodbrok or Ragnarr Loðbrók which means "Ragnar Hairy Breeches" in Old Norse) was a legendary Norse ruler and hero whom became known as the scourge of England and France. He was said to be the son of Sigurd Hring, a King of Sweden and succeeded the throne upon his father's death.

Ragnar Lothbrok had been married three times. His first wife was **Lagertha**, whom he had met in a battle while avenging his grandfather's death, King Siward. King Frø of Sweden invaded Norway and killed the Norwegian King Siward.

To add insult to injury for public humiliation, King Frø ordered that the surviving women of King Siward's family into a brothel. When Ragnar Lothbrok heard about King Frø's invasion of Norway, he came with an army to avenge the death of his grandfather.

When Ragnar arrived, some of the women King Frø had ordered into the brothel dressed in men's clothing and helped fight on Ragnar's side. Among these women dressed as men and fighting in front among the bravest was the skilled shield-maiden Lagertha.

Lagertha fought as ferociously as a man and only the loose locks of her hair flowing over her shoulders revealed her as being a women. This impressed Ragnar greatly and lead him to court her. Lagertha pretended to be interested in his proposals and Ragnar came to seek her hand in marriage.

However when he arrived, Lagertha had a bear and a great hound which were guarding her home, attack Ragnar when he arrived. He killed the bear with his spear and choked the hound to death. By doing this, he won Lagertha's hand in marriage. Ragnar had three children with her, a son named Fridleif and two daughters (whose names are lost to history).

Unfortunately, Ragnar continued to hold a grudge

against Lagertha for having her two beasts attack him when he originally sought out her hand in marriage and divorced her and returned to Denmark.

When he returned to Denmark, Ragnar was faced with a civil war and sent word to Norway for support. Lagertha, whom still loved him, heeded his call and came to his aid in Denmark with 120 ships full of warriors. Lagertha arrived with her ships of warriors and saved the day for Ragnar with a counterattack by circling around and attacking the enemy from the rear. She took Ragnar's enemies by surprise and turned the tide of the battle, causing their opponents to panic.

Upon returning to Norway, she quarreled with her new husband (*name unknown*) and slew him with a spearhead that she had concealed in her gown. She then usurped the whole of his name and sovereignty, as she found it better to rule without her husband than to share the throne with him.

Ragnar Lothbrok's second wife was the daughter of King Herrauðr of Sweden, Thora Town-Hart (Þóra borgarhjörtr). King Herrauðr had acquired an egg from Bjarmland (Arkhangelsk Oblast, Russia, next to Finland). The egg had hatched into a lindworm (wyrm or dragon) and grew into a great serpent that encircled her bower (apartment). Her father promised Thora's hand in marriage to whomever could slay this great serpent. This is when Ragnar famously wore the hairy breeches that gained his nickname, "Lothbrok" (Loðbrók) which means "Hairy-Breeches."

Ragnar went to Västergötland (West Gothland, in Southwest Sweden) where her bower was located and dressed himself in shaggy clothes and the hairy beeches that he treated with tar and sand to protect him from the serpent's poison. He took a spear and approached the serpent which spewed poison at him, but Ragnar protected himself with his shield and was also protected by his tar and sand treated clothes. He speared the serpent through its heart and cut off its head. married Thora.

Thora gave Ragnar two sons Eiríkr (Erik) and Agnar, whom later died of an illness.

The name of Ragnar's third wife was Aslaug (Aslög). Aslaug was said to be the daughter of the legendary Norse hero Sigurd (Old Norse: Sigurðr) and the shield-maiden Brunhild (also spelled Brynhildr or Brünnhilde). Upon the deaths of her parents, Sigurd and Brunhild, she was then raised by Brunhild's foster father Heimer. However, Heimer was concerned about Aslaug's safety and kept her identity hidden. Legend states that he built a large harp to hide her in and traveled as a poor harp player, keeping the girl concealed within it.

They arrived at Spangereid at Lindesnes in Norway, where they stayed for the night in the house of the peasants Åke and Grima. Åke believed that the mysterious large harp contained valuables and told his wife Grima about it. Grima then convinced him to murder Heimer while he was sleeping. However, after they murdered Heimer and broke the harp open, they discovered the hidden little girl, whom they named Kråka ("Crow") and raised as their own child.

In order to hide her beauty, the accepted sign of her noble origins, they rubbed her in tar and dressed her in a long hood.

However, one day when as she was bathing, she was discovered by some of Ragnar Lothbrok's men, whom were confused by Kråka's beauty and allowed the bread they were baking to burn as they watched her. When Ragnar inquired about the mishap with the bread, they informed him about the beautiful girl they'd seen.

Ragnar then sent for her and to test her wits,
he commanded her to arrive
neither dressed nor undressed,
neither hungry nor full,
and neither alone nor in company.

To this challenge, Kråka arrived dressed in a net, biting an onion, and with only a dog as her companion.

Ragnar's challenge to test Kråka's wits.

Ragnar was genuinely impressed by her ingenuity and felt that she would be a wise companion. Ragnar proposed marriage to her, but she refused until he'd accomplished his mission in Norway.

When Ragnar visited Östen Beli, the viceroy of Sweden, he had told him of the maiden Kråka (Aslaug), but Östen persuaded him to reject Kråka and instead to marry Ingeborg, a Swedish princess. On Ragnar's return home, "three birds" had already informed Kråka of his plans to marry the princess Ingeborg and so she expressed her disapproval of this to him and revealed to him her true noble origins. In order to prove she that she was indeed the daughter of the hero Sigurd whom had slain the dragon Fafnir, she told him that she'd bear him a child whose eye would bear the image of a serpent.

Fulfilling this, she bore him a son whom had the image of a snake encircling the pupil and he was named Sigurd "Snake-in-the-Eye." When Östen learned of Ragnar's change of plans to marry the princess Ingeborg, he rebelled against him but was slain by Ragnar's sons at Kråka's (Aslaug) bidding.

Aslaug (Kråka) bore Ragnar four more sons: Ivar the Boneless, Björn Ironside, Hvitserk, and Ragnvald.

Although these marriages were recorded consecutively in history/lore, Ragnar Lothbrok was a bit of a ladies' man and shared the beds of all three, Lagertha, Thora and Aslaug. Each bearing children to him before being married, because there is mention of the deeds of Ragnar's sons before he was betrothed to their mothers.

Ragnar's sons grew up and set out to prove themselves as equals to their father. They made wars far and wide and conquered such places as Zealand, Reidgotaland (Jutland), Gotland, Öland and all the surrounding small islands. Ivar, whom was the cleverest, was their leader and installed himself at Lejre on the island of Zealand, East Denmark.

Ragnar's sons grew to be strong warriors of their own accord and became even more ambitious. Ragnar didn't want his sons to overshadow him and seek his kingdom from him. So he appointed Eysteinn Beli to be the king of

Sweden in his stay and instructed him to protect it from his son's ambitions.

One summer when Ragnar was out Viking (pillaging) in the Baltic region, his two sons from Thora, Erik (Eiríkr) and Agnar, came to Lake Mälaren in Sweden seeking the kingdom. They send a messenger to Gamla Uppsala, which is the seat of Swedish Kings and a place in Sweden that hosted regular sacrificial rites and royal burials, and asked King Eystein to meet them.

Upon his arrival, they demanded that the King be their vassal and to give his daughter Borghild to Erik to be his wife. When King Eystein heard their demands, he consulted the Swedish chieftains and they made the decision to attack Erik and Agnar. After a long battle against overwhelming numbers, the brothers lost against the Swedish forces. Agnar was slain in the battle, but Erik survived the battle and was captured alive.

King Eystein desiring peace and wanting to seal a peace treaty went ahead and offered his daughter to Erik and as much from the *Uppsala öd* as he wanted. The *Uppsala öd* was the ancient collection of royal estates that financed the Swedish Kings.

But Erik declined the King's offer and stated that he didn't wish to live after such a humiliating defeat. The defeated Erik asked the King to be raised him up on the points of spears above the slain in the battlefield, so he'd be pierced by the spears and slain on the field of battle.

He wished to be put to death in this manner so he could enter Valhalla with the rest of the battlefield's slain. A demand which, the Swedish rulers granted. This was the end of Ragnar Lothbrok's sons by Thora.

In 850 AD, Dane Vikings overwintered for the first time on the Isle of Thanet near Kent, England. Usually they went home to winter and returned to England in the warmer summer months to raid. They were securing areas now where they felt safe to winter over.

After the year 851 AD, Norsemen began to also stay in the lower Seine Valley of Francia for the winter as they began to secure a better hold of the area. This was occurring also in Kent, Scotland, and in Ireland as Norsemen began to stay throughout the year. In Ireland near Waterford for example, the Norse had established a more permanent settlement in 853 AD. Viking raids were intensifying everywhere the Norse could reach and their reach was fast expanding.

By 854 AD a raiding party overwintered a second time, at the Isle of Sheppey in the Thames estuary, where the River Thames runs into the North Sea and by the following year in 855 AD, the Isle of Sheppey became a regular wintering camp for the occupying Danes. The unguarded River Thames provided a convenient gateway for Viking raiders seeking island targets and also as a entrance port from the mainland reaching into Francia.

The raids following the rivers and hitting inland Francia became more regular. By 858 AD, Vikings had captured and burned Chartres, Francia. They did it twice more in the 860's AD. Vikings simply rowed to Paris and left only when they acquired sufficient loot or were bribed by the Carolingian rulers. These Viking raiders are believed to have been led by none other than Ragnar Lothbrok himself.

The Viking raids by these invading Norsemen were getting so frequent and bad that by 862 AD, the King of West Francia, Charles the Bald (later known as Charles II) had to put a stop to it.

Portrait of Charles the Bald (823-877).[56]

King Charles II put a stop to much of the raiding by defending his rivers and fortifying his towns. By doing so, he effectively made it more difficult for the Vikings to easily raid or attack. Many religious communities and monasteries were moved inland and out of reach from Viking opportunists, this eliminated the easy pickings by raiders.

By this time, many Norsemen had already settled in Shetland, Orkney, the Hebrides and Man, and parts of mainland Scotland. These Norse settlers were to some extent integrating with the local Gaelic population in the Hebrides Islands and the Isle of Man. These areas were ruled over by local Norse Jarls that were originally captains of ships.

Hersirs were Norse leaders that were followed by large bands Viking raiders that also claimed the land where they settled and occupied. The Jarl of Orkney and Shetland however, claimed supremacy over all of the Isles with the other Jarls or Hersirs under him.

"King Rorik"[47]

With Francia becoming increasing more difficult to raid, Viking bands diverted their attention more on England. In 864 AD they reverted to the Isle of Thanet for their winter encampment before conducting summer raids.

Desiring to show himself as a better warrior than his sons, Ragnar Lothbrok decided to conquer England with only two knarr ships. Knarrs were a type of merchant ship used by the Norse traders at the time. The ships Ragnar had were built in Vestfold, Norway and were indeed enormous ships.

Ragnar's wife, Aslaug didn't approve of this idea because such large ships weren't fit for attacking the English coast, only the more maneuverable longships were more capable for that task. However, Ragnar refused to heed her advice and arrived safely with his army in England and began a campaign to ravage and burn his way across the country.

Sometime late in 864 or early 865 AD, Ragnar had made his way to Northumbia and became shipwrecked off the coast. Hearing the news of Ragnar being shipwrecked, King Ælla of Northumbria mustered an overwhelming force and defeated Ragnar's army while they were vulnerable. They were able to take Ragnar alive and held him prisoner. King Ælla, mocking the tales he'd heard of Ragnar's immunity to snakes during the time when he courted Thora and slew the serpent, had Ragnar Lothbrok thrown into the snake pit.

King Ælla having Ragnar Lothbrok put to death in a pit of snakes.[48]

However, it is said that Ragnar was protected by an enchanted silken shirt that Aslaug had made for him. It was only when this shirt had been removed from him that the snakes were able to bite Ragnar and kill him with their venom.

Before 865 AD, most Viking raids were predominately hit and run operations, but by that year in 865 AD they changed into invasions with the intent to conquer. It is believed that pressure from tyrannous kings in Nordic regions forced them to seek new lands and start new lives. Norsemen were now looking for farm land to settle their families.

The legend in the Sagas of Ragnar's Sons (Ragnarssona þáttr) claims that some of the attention of England by Ragnar Lothbrok's sons was because of the death of their father, Ragnar Lothbrok whom was killed by the king of Northumbria, Ælla, during a raid in which Ragnar was taken prisoner and thrown into a snake pit. The following

55

year, Ragnar's sons build a substantial force and sought vengeance for their father against King Ælla.

In 865 AD, the **Great Heathen Army**, otherwise known as the **Great Viking Army** was formed by uncoordinated bands of Norse Vikings that came from Denmark, Norway, and Sweden. They were led by Ragnar Lothbrok's sons, Ivar Ragnarsson (Ivar the Boneless), Halfdan Ragnarsson (Halfdene), and Ubbe Ragnarsson (Hubba), along with the Dane Viking chieftain Guthrum.

The Norsemen were well aware of the civil war that had weakened the great northern kingdom in England and as warriors these Norse were extremely opportunistic.

The Norse consolidated their forces as they came in and wintered in East Anglia. To protect their realm and as an opportunity to see their rivals in Northumbria attacked, East Anglia made a peace agreement with the Norse army. They allowed the Norse to use their lands to gather their army and provided them with horses. The Norse used it as a staging point for their invasion into Northumbria.

By late 866 AD, the Great Heathen Army marched into Northumbria and on November 21st they seized York, which they called Jórvik. York (Jórvik) had a great defensive and was a strategic stronghold that was well protected by the walls the Roman Army had built for it previously.

Kings Ælla and Osberht united their forces and made an attempt to retake York months later on March 21st 867 AD. But two days later on March 23, 867 AD, as they continued their attempt to retake York from the Great Heathen Army, the battle ended when King Osberht was killed and King Ælla was captured. King Ælla was horrifically subjected to traditional Norse warrior practice of the Blood Eagle ordeal by having his ribs torn out and folded back to form the shape of an eagle's wings.

Routes taken by the Great Heathen Army from 865 to 878 AD.[57]

Reputedly, it was punishment for King Ælla's alleged murder of Ragnar Lothbrok by throwing him into a pit of snakes after his failed raid on Northumbria the prior year.

After that battle and the Norse seizing control of the region, the Northumbrians paid the Vikings off and the Great Heathen Army's collected leaders established as King in their place, Egbert (Ecgberht I). King Egbert was put in place to be a puppet leader and tax collector in Northumbria. The Great Heathen Army then set off for the Kingdom of Mercia, where in 867 AD they captured Nottingham.

King Burgred, the king of Mercia and Kent, requested help from his brother-in-law King Æthelred I, the king of Wessex, to help in defense against the Viking invaders.

King of Mercia Athelred seen on the exterior of Lichfield Cathedral.[51]

King Æthelred and his brother Alfred, the future Alfred the Great, led a West Saxon army from Wessex and Mercia and besieged the Norse occupied city of Nottingham with no clear result. The Mercians settled on paying the Vikings off to leave instead.

The Vikings of the Great Heathen Army returned to Northumbria in the Autumn of 868 AD and stayed the winter in York,. They remained in York for most part of the year 869 AD. Some remained in hopes of starting a new life in York, but most sought land of their own. It was the main reason they'd come in the first place and their leaders reassured them there was more areas available.

The Great Heathen Army returned to East Anglia and spent the winter of 869/870 AD at Isle of Thetford. This time when the Norse arrived there wasn't a peace agreement between the East Anglians and the occupying Viking army. The East Anglians weren't caught by surprise this time and the Great Heathen Army wasn't as numerous as before either. They seen this as an opportunity to repel the Norse invaders from their land, so the local King Edmund fought against the Norsemen to no avail. He was captured and killed. Subduing the East Anglians, the Great Heathen Army wintered there and prepared to attack further Anglo lands as soon as weather permitted,

The Battle of Englefield was a battle that took place on New Years Eve, December 31st, 870 AD at Englefield near Reading, which is now the English county of Berkshire. It was one of a series of battles that took place following an invasion of the then Kingdom of Wessex by an army of

Danes. During these battles in which the Danes had established a camp at Reading. Both the battle and campaign are described in the Anglo-Saxon Chronicle.

Three days after their arrival in Reading, a party of Danes, led by two of their jarls, rode out towards Englefield. It was here that Æthelwulf, the Ealdorman of the shire, had mustered a force and was waiting for them. In the ensuing Battle of Englefield, many of the Danes, including one of the jarls named Sidrac, were killed while the rest of the Danes were driven back to Reading.

A battle between 'Anglo-Saxons' and 'Vikings' staged by re-enactors.[50]

However, the Saxon victory at Englefield did not last long. Four days later the main West Saxon army, led by King Ethelred and his brother, Alfred the Great attacked the main Danish encampment at Reading and were bloodily repulsed. This battle became known as the First Battle of Reading. Among many of the dead on both sides was Æthelwulf, whom had repelled the invading Norse in the first place.

In 871 AD, King Bagsecg came to England from Scandinavia and brought with him the **Great Summer Army.** He arrived and added his forces to the Great Heathen Army which had already had much success in overruning much of England.

King Bagsecg and Halfdan Ragnarsson dispatched a few raiding parties to attack the Kingdom of Wessex which remained vulnerable to Viking style raids and they captured Reading and Berkshire where they set up camp within the towns. On January 4th, 871 AD, Alfred attempted to attack the camp, however Bagsecg won a great victory at what's called *The Battle of Reading* where he inflicted terrible losses on Prince Alfred's army.

Reenactors depicting King Alfred with the West Saxon (Wessox) forces battling the Danish Norsemen of the Great Summer Army.[52]

The Battle of Ashdown, in Berkshire (possibly the part now in Oxfordshire), took place on January 8th, 871 AD. Both forces met for battle on the North Wessex Downs in Berkshire. The Vikings horde were commanded by Bagsecg and Halfdan and five other Danish Jarls. The Viking army itself was outnumbered in comparison to the West Saxons led by Alfred. This battle would determine the fate of Wessex and its king.

Alfred's elder brother King Æthelred of Wessex was busy praying in a church and refused to fight until his other army arrived. This left Alfred in command and the West Saxon and Viking armies met and the battle itself lasted all day. King Bagsecg was killed along with his five Danish Jarls.

According to the Anglo-Saxon Chronicle, King Bagsecg was slain by a sword while Halfdan fled from the field of battle with the rest of the army back to Reading.

The Battle of Ashdown itself was a limited West Saxon Victory, because two weeks later they would meet the Norsemen on the battlefield again.

The Battle of Basing was a battle that took place on January 22nd in the year of 871 AD at Old Basing in what is now known as the English county of Hampshire. It was one of a series of battles that took place following an invasion of the then kingdom of Wessex by an army of Danes. These Dane Norse were remnants of the merged Great Heathen Army and Great Summer Army.

The Danes had established a camp at Reading and the previous battles of Englefield, the Battle of Reading and the Battle of Ashdown, had proved indecisive with victories to both sides.

Two weeks after following the costly Saxon victory at Ashdown, King Æthelred and his brother Alfred were forced to retreat their army to Basing, where the two armies met again. The Saxon army led by King Æthelred was beaten by the Dane forces led by Ivar the Boneless (Ingvar). However, just like the preceding battles, this battle was also indecisive and two months later was followed by the Battle of Marton that happened on March 22nd, 871 AD where the Saxons prevailed.

These were the last known battles to be fought by King Æthelred against the Danes that year and the King is reported to have later died shortly later on April 15th, 871 AD.

Whether he died in battle or died shortly afterward on April 23rd as a result of wounds he suffered in battle is unclear.

Ether way, King Æthelred died and was succeeded by his younger brother Alfred, whom later became known as Alfred the Great. King Alfred inherited both the throne of Wessex and its immediate need of defense against the Norse invaders.

The English continued to suffer defeats and after the defeat at Wilton, King Alfred's optimism that he'd be able to defend his kingdom from the Norsemen was deteriorating and he was forced to make peace with them. The terms of this peace agreement are unknown, but the Norse withdrew from Reading in the Autumn of 871 AD and wintered in London before returning to Northumbria in 872 AD.

The Northumbrians had rebelled against the puppet leader previously installed by the Norse, so the Great Heathen Army returned to restore power and then wintered in Lindsey for the winter of 872-873 AD. The Mercians continued to pay off the Viking invaders in exchange for peace and the Norse took up quarters in Repton for the following winter of 873-874 AD.

The following year in 874 AD, the Great Heathen Army conquered Mercia and drove the Mercian King Burgred into exile, placing the Mercian, Ceolwulf II, in power as a puppet leader and demanded oaths of loyalty.

After the Vikings had conquered the Kingdom of Mercia, the Great Heathen Army had split in two with half of the Viking army following Halfdan Ragnarsson whom led his band north into Northumbria and then wintered by the River Tyre. Following the winter of 875 AD, he led his Viking band North to battle the Picts and Britons in the Kingdom of Strathclyde.

The year following in 876 AD, Halfdan then returned South and shared out the land with the other Norsemen in a region that became known as **The Danelaw.**

The Danelaw was the land conquered in England by the Great Heathen Army and then was occupied by the remaining Norsemen that settled there. This region fell under the Norse laws followed by the occupying Viking

Danes.

The second band of Vikings in the Great Heathen Army which were led by Guthrum, Oscetel, and Anwend, had left Repton in 874 AD and established a base camp at Cambridge for the winter of 874–875 AD. In the late of 875 AD, this band of Vikings moved on to Wareham, where they raided the surrounding areas and then occupied a fortified position to secure it. However, King Alfred of Wessex made a treaty with this group of Norsemen and they agreed to leave the Realm of Wessex. Nevertheless, it wasn't long until they started raiding other parts of Wessex and forced King Alfred to take up arms and fight back again.

Statue of King Alfred at Wantage holding an ax.[53]

By 876 AD, the Viking King Guthrum (Guðrum) had acquired various parts of the Kingdoms of Mercia and Northumbria and was now turning his attention to acquiring the Kingdom of Wessex, where his first confrontation with Alfred had taken place on the southern coast. The Viking King Guthrum sailed his army around Poole Harbour and linked up with another Viking army that was invading the area between the Frome and Trent rivers which were also ruled by King Alfred.

King Guthrum had won his initial battle against King Alfred and he'd successfully captured the Castellum as well as the ancient square where a convent of nuns was located that is known as the Wareham.

King Alfred then negotiated a peace settlement with the Viking invaders, but by 877 AD this peace agreement was broken when King Guthrum led his Viking army to raid further into the Wessex realm.

This action forced King Alfred to confront the Vikings in a series of skirmishes that King Guthrum continued winning. After King Guthrum had successfully captured Exeter, King Alfred was forced to seek a peace treaty that resulted in King Guthrum leaving the Kingdom of Wessex to winter in Gloucester.

The peace treaty lasted until on the night of 6th January 878 AD, King Guthrum made a surprise attack in the darkness on King Alfred and his court at Chippenham, Wiltshire. It was the Christian feast day of Epiphany and the Anglo Saxons were taken by surprise by the Vikings. However, it's also possible that Wulfhere, the Ealdorman of

Wiltshire, had allowed the attack because when King Alfred returned to power later that year, he stripped Wulfhere of his role as Ealdorman.

King Alfred was forced to flee from the attack with a few retainers and took shelter in the marshes of Somerset where they stayed in the small village of Athelney.

King Alfred spent the next few months building up his force while waging a guerrilla war against King Guthrum's secured refuges located in the fens. After a few months King Alfred was able to call forth men loyal to him to Egbert's Stone, where they then traveled to Ethandun and fought the Viking invaders that were led by King Guthrum.

This fighting went on until King Alfred was eventually able to defeat the half of the Viking Great Heathen Army led by King Guthrum in the Battle of Edington in May of 878 AD.

At the battle, King Alfred had routed the remains of King Guthrum's band from the Great Heathen Army. The Viking remains fled to their encampment and King Alfred sieged them for two weeks until eventually defeating them and making the Peace Treaty of Wedmore.

The peace treaty was made and the Viking King Guthrum was baptized as a Christian and assumed the new christening name of Æthelstan. Guthrum, now known as Æthelstan converted his faith while also accepting King Alfred as his godfather.

This treaty had established peace between the two rulers and also clearly defined the borders between the realms of

King Alfred and King Æthelstan (Guthrum).

The Kingdoms of Wales was not colonized by the Vikings as heavily as eastern England, Scotland, Ireland, and the surrounding Isles were. The Vikings did, however, settle in the South around St. David's, Haverfordwest, and Gower, among other places.

These were fairly easily accessible locations that could be reached by boat. The Vikings did not subdue the Welsh mountain kingdoms because they were not as easily accessible by waterways that the Vikings were so accustomed to and a dwindling army the Norse were now from previous engagements. The remains of the Great Heathen Army that swiftly conquered much of England, Scotland, Ireland, and the surrounding isles was now broken up and scattered into separate areas.

The Viking son of Halfdan the Black, Harald Fairhair (also known as Harald Halfdansson or Harald Hårfagre) was born in the Petty Kingdom of Rygjafylke in 850 AD. This located in what is called Rogaland, Norway today.

He was the son of Halfdan the Black, who was King of Vestfold (a petty kingdom) and a member and heir of the House of Yngling (a legendary Swedish royal clan with kings, which includes Ragnar Lodbrok, that is also mentioned in the Sage of Beowulf).

When King Halfdan the Black died, Harald Fairhair became the sovereign of several small and scattered petty kingdoms in Vestfold, Norway that his father had acquired through conquest and inheritance.

Statue of the first King of Norway, Harald Hårfagre (Fairhair).[54]

King Harald Fairhair went on to unify Norway and became the first King of Norway as a result. The unification of Norway began from a rejection of King Harold's marriage proposal from Gyda, the daughter of King Eirik, King of Hordaland (a petty kingdom in southern Norway).

When he proposed marriage to her, she is said to have refused to marry King Harald unless he was King of all of Norway. Upon this, Harald took a vow to never comb or cut his hair until he was the sole king over all of Norway.

In 866 AD, King Harald began a series of conquests against the several petty kingdoms of Norway until in 872 AD, after a great victory at the Battle of Hafrsfjord, when King Harald (now known as King Harald I of Norway) became the sole ruler of a now unified Norway.

However, not everyone shared King Harald's enthusiasm for a unified Norway nor of King Harald being the sole ruler of it. As a result his realm of the now unified Norway became under constant threat from many opponents that were forced to flee Norway and seek refuge in either Iceland, the Orkney Islands, Shetland Islands, Hebrides Islands, Faroe Islands, Scotland, Ireland, Northumbria, Mercia, or in the northern European mainland in what became Normandy.

This explains the sudden surge of the numbers that were so easily added to the Great Heathen Army and the increase in the number of Viking expeditions appearing along, just about every coastline in Northern Europe and the Isles in general. This was because of King Harald I of Norway and leaving wasn't entirely voluntary because many Norwegian chieftains whom were wealthy and respected were perceived as a threat by King Harald Fairhair. They were therefore subjected to much harassment from King Harald and by those loyal to him. This prompted them to vacate their lands and seek refuge in Iceland, the isles and mainlands of Ireland, Scotland, and England.

Most of the Viking invasions of the 9th Century were not acts of piracy, but acts of necessity and desperation as many

Norse had suddenly become homeless and were forced to seek out new places to settle. This was when the Viking raids changed into Viking invasions and permanent occupation.

In 875 AD, King Harald Fairhair sent a fleet from Norway to Scotland in an attempt to unite it with the Kingdom of Norway. He had discovered that many of the Norse that were opposed to his rising power and unification of Norway had fled there. Many of them had taking refuge in the Isles by Scotland.

From these locations in the Isles, his opposition were launching raids and attacking Norway itself. To deal with this problem he organized a fleet that was led by Ketill Bjornsson (Ketill Flatnose) to subdue the Norse rebels and bring the rebellious independent Jarls under the control of his Kingdom of Norway. Many of the Norse rebels that had fled to Iceland were attacking Norway as well.

King Harald's commissioned fleet had successfully subdued the Norse rebels on the Isles and King Harold then found himself ruling not only Norway, but now the Isles of Man and parts of Scotland of which he annexed into the Kingdom of Norway.

However, Ketill Bjornsson, who been sent to subdue the rebels and seize the lands on the King of Norway's behalf, had decided to claim the captured Isles for himself and thus sent no tribute to King Herald of Norway.

Because of this betrayal, King Harald seized the possessions of Ketill Bjornsson that were in Norway and also banished Ketill's sons from Norway as well. The

Viking Ketill and his family was now outlawed and fearing the bounty put on his head Ketill decided to flee to Iceland, where most of his family eventually migrated with him as a result of King Harald of Norway actions against him.

It was Ketill's grandson, who was the son of Olaf the White King of Dublin, that sought loyalty to the King of Norway and invaded Scotland to extract tribute from nearly half the kingdom until his eventual death in battle.

Map of England 878 AD.[10]

By 879 AD, Guthrum's remaining army left Wessex, with some following him to his new Kingdom and some leaving to live a more settled life in York, Northumbria. Some assembled on the Thames to form a new army to return to the European continent to begin new campaigns and take advantage of the political turmoil in Francia with the death of King Charles the Bald (Charles II) in 877 AD.

Although with the treaty in place between King Alfred of Wessex and King Guthrum of the Danelaw, Alfred was saved any major conflicts but still had to deal with the occasional Viking raid here and there upon his kingdom. Alfred had reorganized his army, rebuilt and built new defenses around the countryside and formed a navy.

Peace between lands of the Danelaw and Wessex continued until in 884 AD when King Guthrum of the Danelaw attacked Wessex. Alfred defeated him and made a peace agreement that was outlined in the Treaty of Alfred and Guthrum. This peace treaty formally drew the boundaries of the Danelaw and allowed for Danish self-rule in that region.

In November 885 AD, a Viking named Rollo (Hrólfr, possibly Ganger Hrolf (Hrolf the Walker)) was one of the lesser leaders of the Viking fleet which besieged Paris under the leadership of Sigfred. The Vikings initially demanded a ransom, but the Count of Paris, Odo denied it to them, even though he could only muster a few hundred soldiers to defend the city. However, even though the Vikings used a variety siege engines, they failed to breach the Parisian Walls. Some of the Vikings left with Sigfred to pillage further up the River Seine. Yet some stayed with Rollo to continue with the siege on Paris and by the following year in October of 886 AD, King Charles the Fat of Francia arrived with his army.

Viking Ships besieging Paris.[55]

To the disappointment to the Parisians, whom had defended the city so tenaciously, King Charles the Fat did not attack the Vikings but instead sent an emissary to find the Viking's chieftain in order to negotiate, but the Vikings replied that they were all chieftains of their own accord.

Eventually he was able to pay them a sum of 700 pounds of silver to leave Paris and allowed them to sail further up the River Seine to pillage Burgundy, which was in revolt at the time.

In 911 AD, the Viking leader Rollo, whom fell foul to the Norwegian King Harald Fairhair, returned to the River Seine with his followers and invaded the area of northern France again. He launched an attack on Paris before laying siege to Chartres. On July 20th 911 AD, Frankish forces were to repel the Viking attack led by Rollo at the Battle of Chartres.

Then on August 26th, 911 AD, after another Frankish victory near Chartres against Rollo's forces, Charles the Simple (King Charles III), whom was now King of Western Francia and of Lotharingia felt Rollo and his army of Norsemen would be worthy allies instead of adversaries and negotiated the Treaty of Saint-Clair-sur-Epte.

In this Treaty, King Charles the Simple in exchange for the Viking's loyalty and pledge of feudal allegiance, gave the city of Rouen and the area of what is present-day Upper Normandy to Rollo and his men in what established the **Duchy of Normandy**, named from the Frankish word for the Viking Men of the North, or Northmen (Normanii).

This was the land between the River Epte and the sea, as well as Brittany, which was an independent country that the Franks had failed to conquer. Additionally, Rollo and his Northmen were to defend the shores of the River Seine.

As a token of goodwill, Rollo also agreed to be baptized Christian as Robert I and to marry King Charles' daughter, Gisela. Legend states that when Rollo was required to kiss the foot of King Charles, as was custom to the condition of the treaty. Rollo refused to perform such a humiliation, in such that when Charles extended his foot to him, he ordered one of his warriors to do so in his place. When his warrior lifted King Charles' foot up to his mouth, it caused the king to lose his balance and fall to the ground.

In accordance to the Treaty of Saint-Clair-sur-Epte, Rollo honored his word and defended the shores of the River Seine. However, Rollo continued to make attacks on Flanders (Modern day Northern Belgium).

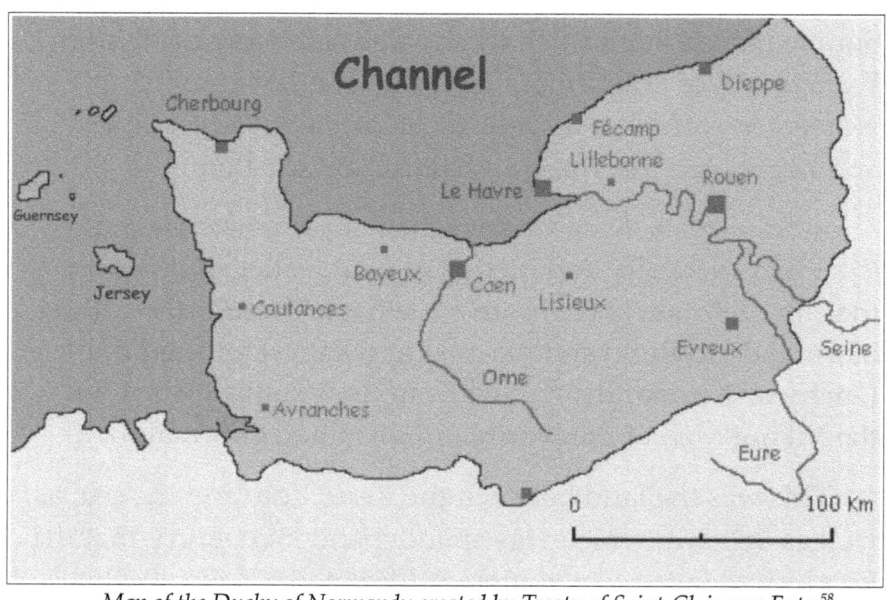

Map of the Duchy of Normandy created by Treaty of Saint-Clair-sur-Epte.[58]

Alfred the Great had died in 899 AD and was succeeded by his son, Edward the Elder. He, along with his sister, Æthelflæd, whom was known as the Lady of the Mercians, conquered several Danish territories in the Midlands and East Anglia in a series of campaigns during the 917 AD. The Danish Jarls who submitted were allowed to keep their lands. Upon the death of his sister in 918 AD, Edward the

Elder also became King of Mercia. At this time, the balance of power in England was shifting out of the hands of the Viking conquerors controlling the Danelaw and into the hands of the Anglo-Saxon King. The Kingdom of Northumbria continued to be ruled by Norsemen.

Robert I of Western Francia, King of the Franks.[59]

In France, King Charles the Simple was deposed of by Robert I in 922 AD. Robert I instilled himself upon the throne as King of Western France, King of the Franks.

Rollo considered his oath to King Charles of France to now be null and voided. The Normans led by Rollo began a period of expansion westwards. In an attempt to stop

77

Rollo's attacks, Frankish Barons made negotiations which ended with Rollo being given Le Mans and Bayeux. Even with the newly gained land, Rollo continued with the seizure of Bessin in 924 AD and the following year Rollo's Normans attacked Picardy.

Rollo statue in Normandy in the town square of Falaise.[61]

In the same year Rollo was attacking Frankish areas, King Edward the Elder died on July 17th, 924 AD while leading an army against a Welsh-Mercian rebellion at Farndon-Upon-Dee. Edward the Elder was then succeeded by his son **Athelstan** (Æthelstan) whom became King of the Anglo-Saxons from the time of his father's death until the year 927 AD when he conquered the remaining Viking hold in York. This victory effectively made King Athelstan the first King of all of England.

British Isles in 10th century.[60]

While England was becoming unified, in Normandy the Viking Rollo began dividing the lands he had conquered between the Epte and Risle Rivers among his chieftains and himself. Rollo then settled in Rouen, making it the capital city of Normandy. In 927 AD, Rollo passed the fief of Normandy to his son William Longsword.

It's uncertain when Rollo died, but he probably lived for a few years after that, but historians are certain that died before the year 933 AD. It is recorded by the historian Adhemar, that Rollo had gone mad towards the end and at one point had 100 Christian prisoners beheaded in front of him to honor the pagan gods whom he worshiped and then later distributed 100 pounds of gold around to the churches in honor of the Christian God he'd been baptized in the Treaty of Saint-Clair-sur-Epte.

Even though Rollo had converted and been baptized as a Christian, as was typical of many converted Norse, he retained the religious roots of Norse beliefs and simply added the Christian god with the rest of his gods, as many polytheists do when converted.

Normandy began to form from a Frankish land once conquered and settled by Norsemen into a land of Norman identified themselves as Normans.

In England during 939 AD, the English King Athelstan died and was succeeded by his son Edmund I. Soon after King Edmund's coronation, he faced military threats from King Olaf Guthfrithson (Olaf III of the Norse-Gael dynasty and also the King of Dublin) whom still laid claim to York which had been conquered by King Athelstan of England.

King Olaf III attacked Northumbria and forced King Edmund I into a treaty which granted King Olaf Northumbria and part of Mercia.

When King Olaf died a couple years later in 942 AD, King Edmund reconquered the Mercian midlands and by 944 AD, took back Northumbria. Two years later in 946 AD, King Edmund himself had died and was succeeded by his brother, King Eadred. Northumbria had once again become unstable until a new wave of Norwegian Vikings appeared in England in 947 AD led by Erik Bloodaxe (Eric Haraldsson). He was the son of King Harald Fairhair of Norway and as soon as he arrived, he'd captured York and claimed Northumbria for himself.

Silver penny of Eric Bloodaxe hailing him as King Eric (Eric Rex). A coin of the last Viking King of York. It circulated during the Viking Age at 947 to 954 AD.[63]

However, King Erik's rule in Northumbria was just as unstable as was when it was in English hands. The Northumbrian's (Scot-Welsh-Norse) loyalty bounced from that of King Edmund (English), to Dublin King Olaf (Norse-Gael), to the Norwegian King Erik (Norse).

Norwegian Viking rule effectively ended in Northumbria when King Erik Bloodaxe was driven out by the Northumbrians in 954 AD.

Note: This is also the year Erik Bloodaxe died, but whether he was slain or killed in battle is not clear. It is possible that he was killed when he was dethroned and expelled from Northumbria, but records point more to him being ambushed and murdered while traveling on an old Roman road.

Erik Bloodaxe was also the last last King of Northumbria. The lands of the former Kingdom of Northumbria were reduced to a Earldom that were disputed between England and Scotland.

By the end of 10th Century, Viking presence in Ireland, Scotland, and England changed from raiders to that of settlers that began to blur into the native population as Norse settlers became permanent inhabitants and effectively became English, Scottish, or Irish.

In 990 AD, Sigurd Hlodvisson (Sigurd the Stout) became the Earl of Orkney and took control of the Hebrides, which he placed a Jarl named Gilli in charge of. It wasn't long before Sigurd faced trouble from his southern neighbors. Earl Finnleik of Moray led an army against him and Sigurd found his men outnumbered seven to one.

Upon the advice of his mother, Sigurd's men carried the Raven Banner (a symbol of Odin) as their battle standard into battle and were victorious. However, as Sigurd's mother had predicted the standard-bearer was killed.

Raven's Banner (hrafnsmerki) as used by Jarl Sigurd.[63]

After a previous period of peace, a series of raids and
attacks had been taking place along the coast of England by
Danish Vikings which were porting in Normandy.
Tensions between England and the Normans became grave
enough that Pope John XV attempted to resolve the conflict
and engineer peace between them. However, this failed
when a sizable Danish fleet began a campaign on England.
It was then after the Battle of Maldon that in 991 AD King
Æthelred II (Æthelred the Unready) was forced into paying
Danegeld (tribute) to the Danish King Sweyn I Forkbeard.

Unfortunately, the tribute paid in Danegold did not stop
the Danish Viking attacks on England. Viking raids
continued along the English coast until in 994 AD, when the
Danish fleet swelled bigger than it was before in 991 AD.
This was when Danish fleet had began attacking while they
headed up the Thames towards London. The battle was
inconclusive and King Æthelred II met with the leaders of

the Danish fleet, of which King Olaf Tryggvason, King of Norway was foremost amongst them.

As a result of the negotiations, 22,000 pounds of gold and silver were paid to the Viking raiders and a peace treaty was signed between King Æthelred II and King Olaf.

In 994 AD King Olaf Tryggvason, whom was already a baptized Christian, was confirmed as a Christian in a ceremony and then after receiving gifts, Olaf made an oath to never come back to England in hostility. After which, King Olaf returned to Norway and never came back to England again. After the peace agreement, some of the Vikings decided to stay in England and entered into King Æthelred II's service as mercenaries, based on the Isle of Wight.

On his way to Norway, King Olav stopped on the Northern Isles to Christianize them by summoning Jarl Sigurd and ordered him, along with all his subjects to be baptized as Christians. Stating that if he refused, he'd have him killed on the spot and would ravage every island with fire and steel. Not surprisingly, Jarl Sigurd agreed to King Olaf's demand of being baptized and the islands converted to the Christian religion in 995 AD.

This was not the end of Viking expansionism. Earlier, **Eric the Red** was expelled from Norway for manslaughter and resettled in Iceland with his family as many Norse refugees from Norway had before him. In 982 AD, the Icelanders had also expelled him at a "thing"(assembly) from Iceland for three years for some killings over a dispute he had committed there.

Erik the Red statue at Qagssiarssuk, Greenland.[64]

This is when Eric the Red made his way to Greenland. Greenland had been discovered previously by Gunnbjörn Ulfsson whom had discovered it by accident when strong winds had driven him to the 'land mass' which he called Gunnbjarnarsker. Later, a Viking named Snaebjörn Galti attempted to settle Greenland, but it had ended in disaster. Eric the Red made the first successful settlement in Greenland. Eric had spent his three years in exile exploring the land. When his time in exile had ended, he returned to Iceland with tales of how great "Greenland" was, giving it the appealing name "Greenland" to lure potential settlers.

After spending the Winter of 985 AD in Iceland, Eric the Red returned to 'Greenland' with a large number of settlers. They established two successful colonies in the only areas suitable for summer farming. Eric the Red's son, Leif

Ericson, explored further West.

In about 985 or 986 AD, Bjarni Herjólfsson, while sailing to Greenland to visit his parents had been blown off course and discovered a land with low lying hills with forests some distance to the West. He did not stop to explore the newly discovered lands, but continued searching for Greenland, eager to see his parents. He eventually found Greenland and then eventually returned to Norway, where he told of this land he had found, but no one showed any interest. It is believed the land he had seen was North America.

Leif Erikson statue in front of Hallgrimskirkja.Iceland.[86]

Fifteen years later in 999 or 1000 AD, Leif Erikson had acquired the ship that Bjarni had sailed with when he spotted the land West of Greenland in hopes of finding the land himself and exploring it. Lief hired a crew of 35 men and set out to find it, following the route in reverse that Bjarni had sailed.

Leif and his crew first landed in a rocky, desolate place that he named "Helluland." meaning "Flat-Rock Land"possibly Baffin Island. They ventured further by sea and landed in a forested place he named "Markland," meaning "Forest Land" possibly Labrador. After sailing at sea for two more days, they landed in a place he named "Vinland." It was at this place where he and his crew built a small winter camp he called Leifsbúðir. After having wintered in the newly discovered settlement in Vinland, Leif returned to the settlement "Brattahlíð" in Greenland during the Springtime with a cargo of grapes and timber. It has believed that the site of Leifsbúðir (Leif's settlement) that is located in L'Anse aux Meadows, Newfoundland (a Canadian province).

In 1004 AD, Leif's brother Thorvald Eiriksson sailed to explore Newfoundland with a crew of 30 men and spent the winter at Leifsbúðir (Leif's camp). In the Springtime, Thorvald attacked nine of the local indigenous people, whom the Norsemen called **"Skrælingar"(Skræling)**, that were sleeping under three skin-covered canoes. One of the victims survived the attack, escaping and came back to the Norse camp with a force. The indigenous people retaliated by attacking the Norse explorers and Thorvald was killed by an arrow that had passed through their defensive barricade. Brief hostilities continued as the remaining Norse explorers stayed through the winter until they left the following Spring.

A depiction of the death of Thorvald Eriksson in North America in 1004 AD.[66]

Thorvald and Leif's brother, Thorstein Ericson along with his wife Guthrith (Gudrida), sailed to the New World to retrieve his dead brother's body. Unfortunately, his expedition got lost and never reached Vinland. Turning back, they returned to Greenland and by the end of the first week of winter they landed at Lysufiord, Norway where Thorstein fell ill and died. The following Spring, his wife Gudrida returned to settlement Greenland of Brattahlíð, called Ericsfiord at the time.

In 1009 AD Thorfinn Karlsefni (Thorfinn the Valiant),

with three ships that contained livestock and 160 (some sources say 250) men and women, sailed south and landed at Straumfjord in Newfoundland. However, they later relocated to Straumsöy, Newfoundland. The Norse settlers began with peaceful relations between the indigenous people (Skræling) as they bartered with furs and gray squirrel skins for milk and red cloth. The Norsemen claimed the natives tied the red cloth around their heads, wearing them as a sort of headdress.

A bull that belonged to Thorfinn Karlsefni came storming out of the wood and frightened the natives so bad that they ran to their skin-covered canoes and fled away. The natives returned in force three days later and attacked the Norsemen. It is said that the natives used a form of catapults where they hoisted a large dark blue sphere on a pole and fired it. When fired, the sphere projectile flew over the heads of the men and made an ugly assortment of noises.

The Norsemen retreated from the native's attack, however Leif Ericson's half-sister Freydís Eiríksdóttir whom was pregnant and unable to keep up with the retreating Norsemen. She called out to her kinsmen to stop fleeing from "such pitiful wretches," claiming that if she had weapons she would do better. At one point, Freydís picked up a sword that belonged to a man whom had been killed by the natives. She pulled one of her breasts from out of her bodice and struck it with the sword she had picked up. This frightened the natives and made them flee.

Meanwhile on the Island of Ireland, disputes over the

lands of Ireland rose as King Brian Boru, the King of Munster, began making moves to be High King of all of Ireland. Political maneuvers and manipulations were taking place and even lands were attacked as he sought to become the High King. Tensions rose to a point that by 1014 AD, King Brian's army was mustered and marching to Dublin to unseat the Irish-Norse King Sigtrygg II Silkbeard Olafsson of Dublin.

King Sigtrygg convinced Brodir of the Isle of Man and Sigurd of Orkney to side with him in the Battle of Clontarf. King Sigtrygg stayed with reinforcements at Dublin while Brodir and Sigurd led the battle that lasted all day. King Brian was killed in the battle, yet the Irishmen prevailed and ultimately drove back their enemies into the sea. Sigurd himself was also killed in the battle, apparently while still holding a Raven banner.

As Britain, the Isles, and the Northern mainland became more settled and prepared to defend themselves against Vikings, other Norsemen sought opportunity in more southerly reaches of mainland Europe, such as Spain. In 1015 AD, a Viking fleet is recorded to have entered the River Minho and sacked the city of Tui Spain. The attack was so devastating that it left the city of Tui abandoned to be later re-established at its current location.

The Norse did not totally give up their designs on England. In 1016 AD, King Cnut the Great became the ruler of the English kingdom, which itself was the product of a resurgent Wessex. With England, Denmark, Norway, and part of Sweden, King Cnut the Great controlled a North Sea

Empire until his death in 1035 AD, when his empire was split up by his successors.

Upon King Cnut's death, the throne of England was succeeded by his son Harold Harefoot until he died in 1040 AD. Upon his death, Harthacnut (another of Cnut's sons) whom was already on the Danish throne, took the English throne, which reunited the previous North Sea Empire of his father, Cnut the Great. However, King Harthacnut only lived another two years after his brother and died in 1042 AD.

At this point in 1042 AD, the monarchy in England reverted back to the English line after being held by the Norse in Danish hands for such a long time. The restored English line's king was Edward the Confessor, whom is known as being the last King of Wessex.

The Norse had still not given up their hopes on ruling over England however. There was a continuing close alliance on the Isles that were tied with the Kingdom of Norway. In the year of 1058 AD, a Viking fleet that was led by the king of Norway's son came united with men and ships from Orkney, the Hebrides, and Dublin to seize the throne of England, but had failed in their attempt.

King Edward the Confessor died in January of 1066 AD without an obvious successor and this caused much controversy as both King Harald of Norway and Duke William of Normandy believed they were the rightful heirs to the throne of England. However, Harald Hardrada (Harald Sigurdsson) also had a claim to be the rightful heir to the throne of England. He landed and attacked with a

Viking army in hopes of taking control of York and thus seize the English crown, but he was defeated and killed at the Battle of Stamford Bridge.

King Harald Hardrada hit in the neck by an arrow at Battle of Stamford Bridge.[49]

This event is often cited as the end of the Viking era as being the last Viking invasion.

However the Viking Era is better marked as coming to a conclusion when the Duke of Normandy, William the Conqueror (also a descendant of Vikings), successfully took the English throne and became the first Norman King of England in the same year of 1066 AD at the Battle of Hastings.

This event of 1066 AD marks the end of the Viking Age. The Norse petty kingdoms became absorbed into countries and the Christian religion spread throughout Europe.

94

Chapter 5 – Norse Religion

It is not known exactly when religion began to form amongst the Norse people, but during the Norse Bronze Age there are suggestions from rock carvings that a semi organized religion began to form during this time. There are depictions of a pair of Twin Gods that were worshiped as well as a Mother Goddess. There is also an association of water sites such as lakes and ponds that were considered holy sites due to items sacrificed and used in ceremonies at these locations such as bronze lurs (a blowing horn without finger holes), jewelry and weapons, animals, and even humans.

There are also rock carvings during the Norse Bronze Age that have some of the earliest depictions of other well known Norse gods, such as a male figure holding an ax or hammer as being the god Thor and others holding spears, possibly depicting the Aesir gods: Odin or Tyr.

One depiction of a Norse Bronze Age rock carving shows a man holding a spear missing a hand which is most probably a depiction of the god Tyr. There is one depiction holding a bow that may be Ullr, the god of bow hunting.

However, it is not known if these are depictions of gods or simply depictions of men holding weapons. Perhaps celebrating a hero in a particular battle or feat that took place.

The religion and beliefs of the Norse people throughout the centuries have deeply rooted their culture into the World around them. Many aspects and influences of their religion and customs exist with us today and have carried into practice with our modern world.

For example, the days of the Week we use today were influenced by Norse religion, customs and beliefs.

Monday, means Moon's Day or Moon Day.

In Old Norse, this day of the week is called: Mánadagr. The first half of the word 'Mána' in Old Norse means 'Moon' and the second half of the word 'dagr' means 'day.' Máni is also the name of the brother of Sól, the Sun. Both whom are being chased by two wolves seeking to devour them.

The translation of the Old Norse word *Mánadagr* for day of the week means in English: *Moon Day*. In modern English we've shortened it to *Monday*.

In German it is called: Montag, Anglo-Saxon: Móndæg, and in Norwegian (Norsk): Mandag.

In a sense when you say Monday, you're not speaking English but a form of Old Norse.

Tuesday is from the Norse's *Tyr's Day*.

In Old Norse this day of the week is called: Týsdagr.

The Old Norse word Týsdagr translates into *Tyr's Day*, in honor of the one handed god Týr. In Anglo-Saxon it is *Tíwesdæg* and in English it's *Tuesday*. The Norwegian word is Tirsdag and in Swedish: Tisdag.

Wednesday is for Odin's Day. In Old Norse this day of the week is called *Óðinsdagr*. Odin was also called Wotan in some areas. This would make the same day of the week called Wotan's Day instead. In the Anglo-Saxon dialect of Norse, this day of the week is called Wódnesdæg (Wotan's Day). In English, *Wódnesdæg* became Wednesday. In Dutch it is called Woensdag.

Thursday is named for Thor's Day, the Thunder God himself. Old Norse this day is: Þórsdagr (Thórsdagr). The Norwegian word for Thor's day is Torsdag and in Anglo-Saxon, it is: Þunresdæg (Thunresdæg).

Friday meaning Frigg or Freyja's Day. The Old Norse day is *Frjádagr*. The Norwegian word for the day is Fredag and in German it is: Freitag. The Anglo-Saxon word for friday is Frigedæg. This is suggesting it to be referencing it as Frigg's day, instead of Freyja's day, which became friday in English from the Old English "Frīge's day." It is suggested that Frigg and Freya were possible the same goddess. The reference to the vanir goddess Freyja didn't spread outside of Scandinavia. Norse settlements outside of Scandinavian regions were commonly referring to Odin's wife, Frigg instead of 'Freyja."

Saturday comes from Saturn's Day. This influence was not from Old Norse, but had Latin influences on the Anglo-Saxons after the 10th century from monks. The Old Norse word for this day of the week is: Laugardagr, which means: Laundering Day. Saturday to the Norse was Washing Day. In Norwegian it is called Lørdag and it's called Laugardagur in Iceland. The English word Saturday came from the Christian church's Latin influence on the Anglo-Saxons whom called it Sæternesdæg. In Dutch. the day is called Zaterdag.

An interesting fact about the Norse is that they were a particularly clean people. This is contrary to beliefs and myths about how savage and unkempt the northern "barbarians" were and how they lived.

The Norse bathed regularly and combed their hair daily. Saturday was the day of the week that they set aside for bathing and washing. This is the reason it is called Launder Day by the Old Norse. An irony to the common misconception that the so called "barbarians from the North" were considered by the rest of the World as being primitively savage in their ways and severely lacked in hygiene.

But it turns out the Norse were cleaner and cared more personal hygiene than that of their critics. Particularly of the criticism of their cleaning habits as was portrayed by christian monks that complained of the Norse's obsessive over cleanliness and their threat of luring christian maidens.

Sunday is Sun's Day. In Old Norse it was called Sunnudagr and is in Norwegian Søndag. The German word is Sonntag and in Anglo-Saxon: Sunnandæg.

Most of the Norse days of the week were so named after

their gods and customs, such as the practice of washing day. These names of the days of the week carried over into modern languages in use today. The old Norse gods may be forgotten to time, but their names live on and are mentioned at least once a week in many Norse influenced languages.

Like all other religions, the Norse had a beginning story and a prophesied dramatic end to the world around them.

The Norse Creation Story

The Story of creation according to the Norse. In the beginning of everything, there was a realm called **Niflheim** (also known as Neflheimr). Niflheim was located on the northern side of the Great Void the Norse called the **Ginunngagap.** The Ginunngagap was the Mighty Gap of nothingness between realms.

Niflheim was a dark and cold place that consisted mostly of ice and frost. Everywhere in Niflheim there was a mist from which it gets its literal translation of its name, 'Mist Home' or 'Mist World.'

In the frozen mist realm of Niflheim, there's a water spring called "Hvergelmir" from which all the cold rivers originate from. The rivers flow down into the Gininngagap where the cold water would then solidify into dense layers of ice. This explained to the Old Norse as to why the North was so cold. It also explained why the rivers and streams that ran down from the mountains was so cold all year long, regardless of season.

The Hvergelmir Spring was believed to be the place from where all living things originated and where they'd eventually return back to after death. Within the spring, it is believed that many snakes live there and that it's the home of the dragon Nidhogg (Old Norse: Níðhöggr).

On the southern side of the Mighty Gap of Gininngagap was the realm of fire called, **Muspelheim**. From the realm of Muspelheim flowed lava and fire that went into the south side of the Gininngagap.

In the center of the Gininngagap, where the ice from Niflheim and the fire from Muspelheim met, formed the great giant **Ymir**. From Ymir more giants formed. As he slept, he'd sweat a giant from each of his armpits, a male and a female. And from his legs, a third giant formed. These giants were the first frost giants (Jötnar *plural*, Jötunn *singular*).

The giants were breastfed by Auðumbla, a giant cow (aurochs possibly) which had also been created in the middle of the great void of the Gininngagap where the Niflheim ice met the fire flowing from Muspelheim.

Daily the great cow Auðumbla would lick the salt from the ice that formed in the Gininngagap for nourishment. One day when she was licking the salt ice, a human hair formed from out of the ice. She continued licking the salt from the ice and on the next day a human head formed from where the human hair had previously formed.

She continued licking the salt ice and then on the third day, a whole human body emerged. This was the first man to have emerged from Auðumbla licking salt from the ice.

Auðumbla licking Búri out of a salty ice-block.[68]

This first man was known as **Buri** and he was also the first of the Aesir Gods.

Buri had a son called Borr that married a frost giant (jötunn) named Bestla and together they had three sons named, Odin, Vili, and Ve. These brothers were to become the creator gods.

The brothers Odin, Vili, and Ve were greatly disturbed by the fact that the Frost Giants (Jötnar) outnumbered the Aesir Gods. The giant Ymir was constantly conceiving new Jötnar and killing Ymir to stop this from happening was the only solution that the three Aesir gods could come up with to solve the problem.

Ymir being slain by the three Aesir gods; Odin, Ve, and Vili.[67]

So they came up with a plan to slay Ymir; While he was sleeping they would attack him.

As soon as they were sure the great giant was asleep, they ambushed him. The slumbering Ymir was instantly rose from his sleep by the attack and there was a huge battle that ensued. The great giant fought with all of his might, but the Aesir gods emerged victorious.

So much blood flowed from the slain great giant Ymir that it drowned most of the Jötnar. All the frost giants died, except Bergelmir and his wife and they escaped to Niflheim. All Jötnar afterward were descended from this frost giant couple.

The Aesir gods dragged the slain body of Ymir to the center of the great void Gininngagap and then Odin, Vili, and Ve, created the World from the slain corpse. From Ymir's blood, they created the oceans and seas. Then they made the mountains from the giant's bones and used his flesh to make the lands. They formed rocks from his teeth and used his hair to make the grass and trees.

From Ymir's eyelashes, the gods made barriers around the World, "**Midgard** (Miðgarð)," where humans would live, to keep it safe from the Jötnar. The clouds formed when they threw his brain into the air and they formed the sky from the great giant's skull. In the sky, they threw some of the sparks that emitted from Muspelheim and those became the stars.

On the splendid plain of Iðavöllr, they then built their home **Asgard**, which was far from the reach of where both the Jötnar and the humans lived.

While Odin, Vili, and Ve were creating everything in the World, worms began crawling out of the dead body of Ymir. These worms turned into and became the dwarfs (dvergr). Odin, Vili, and Ve told four of the dwarfs to hold up the sky, as they didn't want to risk the sky falling down.

The names of the four dwarves holding the sky were: 'Nordi' (North), 'Vestri' (West), 'Sundri' (South), and 'Austri' (East). The rest of the dwarves made their homes in Nidavellir, which was underground in the rocks and caves where the dwarves became expert craftsman and builders.

Two dwarfs as depicted in the 19th century by Lorenz Frølich.[69]

104

A Jötunn (frost giant) had two children that were so beautiful that they actually shined. So the frost giant called his bright son 'Mani' (Moon) and his radiant daughter 'Sol' (Sun). The children were admired by the whole world and this was a source of great pride to the Jötnar.

The Aesir gods became furious by this arrogance and took both of them from him and placed them in the sky. Sol (Sun) and Mani (Moon) were then pulled across the sky by horse driven chariots.

"The Wolves Pursuing Sol and Mani" by J.C. Dollman 1909.[70]

To keep the Sun and Moon's motion constant and swift, the Aesir gods placed two other Jötunn children named, Sköll and Hati (Hati Hróðvitnisson) in pursuit behind them. These two Jötunn children in pursuit were both great wolves and they chased Sol (Sun) and Mani (Moon) in a never ending quest to gobble them whole.

Each month wolf Hati was able to take a bite out of the Moon, trying to gobble it up as it caught up to it. But the Moon always got away and grew whole again after a few days. At Ragnarok, the wolves Sköll and Hati would eventually catch the sun and the moon and consume them whole.

Until that time happens in Ragnarok, the Norse end of times, the chase after the Sun and the Moon goes on relentlessly.

The three Aesir gods, Odin, Vili and Ve, were walking on a beach one day when they came upon two logs. One log was from an Ash tree and the other from an Elm tree. From these two logs, the Aesir gods created the first humans.

From the Ash log became the first man, named **Ask** and from the Elm log became the first woman named **Embla**.

The Aesir gods gave them life by each giving them separate gifts. Spirit and life were given from Odin. Ve gave both logs movement, mind and intelligence. And from Vili they were given shape, speech, feelings, and the five senses. The Aesir gods decided that the humans should live in the place they created named Midgard.

Midgard would be the garden of mankind of which the gods had created, both humankind and their world around them.

The first living people, Ask and Embla. Sölvesborg, Sweden.[71]

To the Norse, there were different realms in which different beings existed and ruled over. They believed there were nine worlds that were divided into three levels.

The 1st level:

>Asgard (Ásgarðr), home of the Aesir (Æsir) gods.

>Vanaheim (Vanaheimr), home of the Vanir (Vanr) gods.

>Alfheim (Ālfheimr), home of the light elves (ljósálfar).

The 2nd level:

>Midgard (Miðgarðr), home of the humans. Midgard is connected to Asgard by the Rainbow Bridge, "Bifrost."

>Jotunheim, home of the Frost Giants (Jötnar).

>Svartalfheim, home of the Dark Elves (dökkálfar).

>Nidavellir, home of the Dwarfs (Dvergr).

The 3rd level:

>Niflheim to the north (underground in Niflheim is Helheim home of the dead).

>Muspelheim to the south, home of the fire Giants and Demons.

In the middle of the nine worlds was the massive ash tree called Yggdrasil (The World Tree) which connected them all by its branches and roots. Yggdrasil had gigantic roots which went in three separate directions to wells in different realms.

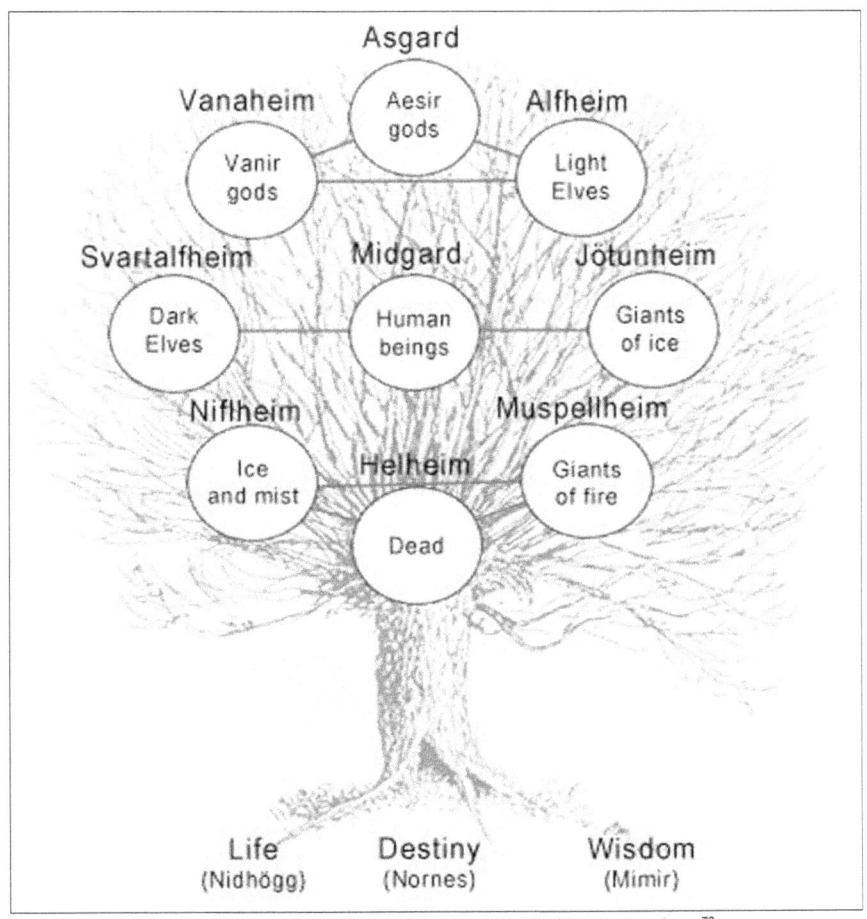

Artist's depiction of Yggdrasil and the nine realms.[72]

The first root from Yggdrasil went to Asgard, the home of the gods. By this root was a well named Urd's well. This was where the Aesir gods held their daily meetings.

The second root from Yggdrasil went down to Jotunheim, the land of the giants, by this root was Mimir's well.

The third root from Yggdrasil went down to Niflheim,

close to the well Hvergelmir. It was here that the dragon Níðhöggr (Nidhug) gnawed on one of Yggdrasil's roots. Níðhöggr was also known to suck the blood out of the dead bodies in Niflheim.

The Norse gods were divided. There were the Aesir gods and the Vanir gods. Additionally, there were the Jotnar (Giants), whom were sometimes counted amongst the Vanir gods. The Aesir were generally considered the warrior gods, while the Vanir gods were the gods of fertility and magic.

Here is a short list of some of the Norse Gods, starting with the Aesir Gods.

Odin (Óðinn), the Allfather, also known as Wotan or Wodan.

Odin the Wanderer by George von Rosen. 1896.[73]

Odin was called the All-Father and was ruler of all the Norse gods and goddesses in all of Asgard. Odin wielded a magical spear called Gungnir that never misses its target and he rode an eight-legged horse named Sleipnir.

Odin sits atop his steed Sleipnir, his ravens Huginn and Muninn and wolves Geri and Freki nearby by Lorenz Frølich. 1895.[74]

The origination of the tale of Odin's stead Sleipnir may have come from Icelandic ponies that have a four-beat lateral ambling gait called a 'super tölt' that makes them appear to have eight legs when using this gait.

Odin was a great seeker of knowledge and even sacrificed one of his eyes at Mimir's Well for wisdow and for the secret of the runes, he pierced himself with a spear and hung from a tree for nine days and nights until the runes revealed themselves to him. He shared the knowledge of the runes with mankind.

Odin Hanging on the World Tree. Illustration by Hans von Wolzogen. 1920.[75]

Odin also has two ravens named Huginn and Muninn, meaning "Thought" and "Memory," whom fly around World each day and then report all the World's happenings to Odin at night.

Odin is usually represented by the Valknut. The Valknut, also known as the Slain Warrior's Knot, is a symbol consisting of three interlaced triangles that are associated with Odin.

The Valknut – The Slain Warrior's Knot of Odin.

Odin is also the god of war, whom often instigates battles by throwing down his spear. Symbolically, in battle Norse have been known to start the conflict by hurling a single spear into the enemy in honor of pleasing the god of war, Odin.

It is Odin, whom commands the Valkyries, the shield maidens that collect the bravest amongst the dead to bring them to the Halls of Valhalla or to the Meadows of Fólkvangr.

Odin was often known to sit on the high seat of Hliðskjálf with his wife Frigg and make wagers with her about the outcomes of events as they looked upon happenings in the other worlds.

The goddess Frigg and her husband, the god Odin, sit on the throne Hliðskjálf and wager the outcome of events.[76]

Frigg, also known as Frigga, was the wife of Odin and the Queen of Asgard, the Realm of the Aesir gods. She is known as being the goddess of foreknowledge and wisdom. Although her husband Odin had many other children, Frigg was the mother of Balder, whom was a god of light and purity. The day of the week Friday is named in honor after this goddess, Frigg's Day.

Balder, also known as Bald, Baldr, Baldor, and Baldur. He was the god of light and purity was the son of Odin and Frigg. Balder has many brothers, which includes the well known gods Thor and Váli. It had been prophesied that the death of Balder would be a sign triggering the event of Ragnarok, so Balder's mother had all things promise to never harm him. This made the god Balder invulnerable to all weapons. This was of great amusement to his brothers and the other gods that would spend hours of entertainment hurling various weapons at him to watch them bounce off of him harmlessly.

Statute of Balder.[77]

Balder was a well beloved, wise, and gentle god whom was accidentally killed when his brother Hod was tricked by Loki into slaying him. Loki had discovered weakness in Balder's invulnerability and used it to trick Hod into slaying him. This event which was a prophesied indication of the coming of Ragnarok. The great war of the gods that would cause the end of times when the World would be destroyed and then recreated.

Thor with Toothgrinder and Toothgnasher.[78]

The god **Thor**, also known as Þórr, Þunor, ðunor, Donar, Thunar, and Þunraz. Thor was a son of Odin and was known as the god of thunder and war. He had red hair and red eyes and was seldom ever without a beard if he could help it. Thor was known as being the strongest of the gods and wielded the hammer, Mjölnir. Thor rode in a chariot that was pulled by two goats named Toothgnasher and Toothgrinder (Old Norse: *Tanngrisnir* and *Tanngnjóstr*).

The hammer wielded by Thor, Mjölnir, was made by the dwarven brothers Sindri and Brokkr. The dwarf brothers were persuaded into a bet by Loki that they couldn't make something better than the things made by the Sons of Ivaldi. The Sons of Ivaldi were the dwarves that crafted special items such as Odin's spear, Gungnir.

The dwarven brothers won the bet by creating Mjölnir, which they presented to Thor. The brothers crafted a fearsome hammer so powerful that it could smash mountains level. The weapon would never fail and if it were thrown, it never missed its intended target. Also when thrown, the hammer would never fly so far that it couldn't return to Thor's hand.

Necklace of Mjöllnir, the hammer of Thor.[79]

The hammer Mjölnir is the religious symbol of Thor and was most commonly worn instead of a cross during a period of resistance by many Norse as a form of defiance against the forced conversions into Christianity.

Thor was revered by warriors, not just because he was a god of war like his father Odin (and some of his brothers), but Thor was one of the strongest gods and was heroically victorious in battle when he fought Jötnar (frost giants).

It was foretold to Odin that Thor would die in the Ragnarök event while battling Jörmungandr, the Great Midgard Serpent. Jörmungandr is the Great Sea Serpent that chases its tail as it encircles Midgard, the realm of mankind.

Circular Symbol of Jörmungandr, The Midgard Serpent.[82]

The symbol of the Midgard Serpent is often depicted as a Serpent chasing its own tail in a complete circle. In Old Norse, the serpent's name is "Jǫrmungandr" and means "huge monster." The venomous serpent is the middle child of Loki and the giantess Angrboða.

Thor had once before encountered the sea serpent Jörmungandr when he was fishing with the reluctant giant Hymir out on a boat. When Hymor refused to give Thor any bait to fish with, Thor chopped off and took the head of Hymir's greatest ox and used that as bait. As Thor was fishing, he caught the great serpent and pulled the beast in with his line as Hymir cowered in the boat of fear.

Thor angling the serpent of Midgard Serpent.81

However as Thor struggled pulling in the beast, the great serpent suddenly broke the line and escaped before Thor could slay it with his hammer, Mjölnir.

Tyr, God of War.[80]

Tyr (Týr), also known as Teiws, Tīw, Ziu, and Tîwaz was also a son of Odin. Tyr was both a god of war and the god of single combat. Tyr was known as the bold one-handed god that lost his hand while tethering the Great Wolf Fenrir. The day of the week, Tuesday is named after this god, "Tīw's Day."

Loki (Luka), also known as Loptr or Hveðrungr, was the son of two giants, Fárbauti and Laufey (or Nál), and was known as the trickster of the gods, His relationship with the Aesir and Vanir gods is a bit hazy as to whether he was a god, a jötunn (giant), or both. Loki is best known for the mischief he caused among the Aesir gods. He is well known as the "trickster-god," even though it is debated as to whether or not he was actually a god or giant.

The Punishment of Loki.[83]

In the Saga "Lokasenna (Loki's Quarrel)," Loki insults the Aesir gods during a feast, each individually, until they become so infuriated that as punishment for his insults and his role in the death of the god Baldr, the gods brought Loki into a cave. Inside the cave, the Aesir gods took three flat

121

stones and drilled a hole in each one of them. The Aesir gods then took two of Loki's sons, Váli and Narfi (or Nari) and changed Váli into a wolf and had him tear apart his brother Narfi. The Aesir then took the entrails of Narfi and bound Loki with them over the three stones they had drilled holes in. They bound his shoulders, his waist, and his lower legs to the three stones. Once Loki was securely bound, the lashings that the Aesir gods had made from Loki's son's entrails were turned into strong iron so he could not escape them.

To add to Loki's torment, Skadi (the god Njord's wife) fastened a venomous snake over Loki so the snake's poison would drip onto his face. Sigyn, Loki's wife, sat with him and held a basin beneath the dripping venom to catch it and prevent it from harming Loki. Yet when the basin would became full, she had to carry the poison filled basin away and empty it. During this time, the poison would drip on to Loki and cause him such pain that he would writhe with such violence that all of the earth shook from the force. Norse legend states that result of Loki's writhing in agony from the poison dripping on him is the result in what are now known as earthquakes.

Loki eventually escapes his bonds during the Ragnarok event and leads the army of dead released from Hel against the Aesir gods.

Mimir (Mímir), also known as Mim was the god of Wisdom. Each day, Mimir drank from a Well (Mimir's Well) with a drinking horn that was made from a dragon's foot and gained great knowledge from it. Mimir arranged the truce between the Vanir and Aesir gods during the Aesir-Vanir war. However, he was beheaded by the Vanir gods when they felt that they had been cheated when the two sides had exchanged hostages to seal the peace.

The Vanir gods sent the head of Mimir to the Aesir gods, whereas Odin preserved it and cast a spell on it so it could speak. Odin then carried the head around to gain counsel, wisdom, and learn secrets from it.

Heimdall (Heimdallr), also known as Hallinskiði, Gullintanni, Vindlér, and Vindhlér. He is described as the "whitest of all gods," has gold teeth, and a golden maned horse named Gulltoppr. He possesses the great horn Gjallarhorn, that will be blown to warn the gods of the coming of Ragnarok.

The Norse god Heimdallr blowing the horn Gjallarhorn.[84]

Heimdall possesses great foreknowledge, keen eyesight, and hearing. He keeps watch at the burning rainbow bridge Bifröst, the link between Midgard and Asgard, guarding the realm of the gods from the Jötnar. Heimdall is believed to be the one whom created the social classes among humans.

Thor's wife, the goddess Sif.[85]

Sif - Thor's wife and the Norse goddess associated with the Earth and Marriage. Sif is known for falling victim to a prank when Loki cuts off her hair and the angered Thor demands that Loki replace it. Loki manages to replace Sif's hair by having the dwarves, the Sons of Ivaldi, create one made of gold for her. Sif's golden hair becomes the first of the six magical items that were made by the Sons of Ivaldi for the gods.

124

Hel – Daughter of Loki, she was appointed by Odin to rule the realm of the dead of which is named after her, "Hel" (Helheim), located in the plane of Niflheim. She is easily recognized because of her gloomy appearance and half black / half flesh colored skin. She takes in the dead whom have died of sickness or old age. The term, "go to hel" is to die and go to her realm.

The goddess Hel.[92]

125

Hod (Höðr), also known as Hoder or Hodur. is another son of the god Odin. Höðr was a blind god that accidentally killed his brother Balder with a weapon made from mistletoe when he was tricked by Loki.

Vidar (Víðarr), also known as Vidar, Vithar, Vidarr, and Vitharr. Vider is the Aesir god associated with vengeance. Víðarr is the son of Odin and the jötunn Gríðr (Grid). Vider avenges his father's death by killing the great wolf Fenrir during the battle at Ragnarök.

Freyr, also known as Frey, Yngvi-Freyr, or Fricco. Freyr is an important Vanir god and is the son of the god Njord. He is associated with farming and weather. Freyr presides over Álfheimr, the realm of the Elves.

The Norse god Freyr standing with his sword and the boar Gullinbursti.[87]

Freyr rides the shining boar Gullinbursti and possesses the best sailing ship, known as Skíðblaðnir, which can be folded and carried in a pouch when not in use. Both items were made by the dwarves (dvargr) known as the Sons of Ivaldi.

Gerda (Gerðr), also known as Gerd or Gerth. Gerda is a jötunn, Vanir Goddess, and the wife of Freyr. She is often known as being a beautiful goddess of fertility and love.

Freyja, also known as Freya, Frejya, Freyia, Frøya, Frøjya, Freia, and Freja. Daughter of Njordr and has a chariot that's pulled by two cats. This Vanir goddess is not only associated with love, beauty, and fertility, but also seiðr (magic), death and war. Freyja rules over Fólkvangr and where she receives half of those whom died in battle (the other half go to Valhalla, Odin's hall).

She also accepts women that have suffered noble deaths into the halls of Fólkvangr. Frayja is also known for her magical cloak of falcon feathers that allows her to fly. She occasionally loans her cloak of feather to the other gods when they're in need of it.

Freyja's married to the Vanir god **Odr** (Óðr), also known as Óð or Od. He is often referred to as the strange double of Odin.

Njord, also known as Njörðr, Njoerd, Njor, or Njorth. He is the father of twins Freyja and Freyr and is the husband of Skadi. Njord is a Vanir god associated with the wind and sea. This makes him a god of fishing, seafaring, and of all things of the sea. He made his home at the sea and lives in Nóatún, which is either his home or his ship.

Njord is one of the gods that survived Ragnarök. He'd been one of the Vanir gods that was traded as a hostage when peace was negotiated between the gods during the Aesir-Vanir War. Njord was often unhappily married as his wife Skadi longed to be in the mountains, whereas Njord long to be by the sea. They had tried to live within each other's realm, but were both unhappy in the other's.

Njord, being with Skadi in her home in the mountains, desires to be by the Sea.[89]

As an act of reparation for Þjazi's death, the Aesir allowed Skadi to choose a husband from amongst them. However, there was a stipulation that she may not see any part of them but their feet when making her choice. She expected to choose Baldr by the beauty of the feet she selected. When she made her choice, Skaði discovered that she had picked Njord.

Skadi (Skaði), also known as Skaoi, Skade, Skathi. Öndurguð, or Öndurdís. Skadi is a jötunn and the goddess associated with winter, the mountains, skiing, and bowhunting. She was married to the god Njord, whom had married her when the Aesir gods allowed her to choose a husband amongst them in return for her dead father.

Skadi longs for the Mountains when with her husband Njord by the sea.[90]

Skadi's home is in the mountains and she's revered by bowhunters whom hope for her blessing in success with their hunts. In the poem *Lokasenna*, she fastens a serpent to drip its venom onto Loki's face when he's bound to rocks as punishment for the death of Baldr by the Aesir gods.

Although she married to Njord, she loved Baldr and was exceptionally bitter towards Loki upon his death.

There are many more other Norse gods, as their children had children and their children's children had children. The Aesir and Vanir gods were a race. They married, reproduced, and even mixed with other races. But they could also be maimed and killed; as could be attested by Odin's one eye, Tyr's missing hand, and the eventual demise of the gods and in the foretold event of **Ragnarok**.

129

Ragnarok

The Twilight of the Gods.

The Norse gods battling at Ragnarok. [88]

Ragnarok (Old Norse: Ragnarøkkr), the Doom of the Gods. This is the great event that was foretold to Odin when many of the gods would die in a great battle fought that would destroy the cosmos in which afterward the World would be again re-created.

The time when the World would be destroyed and then rebuilt was prophesized by a Völva (Seeress) to the god Odin. He was told when the first events would come to pass and informed the other gods, whom started preparing and taking steps to prevent or at least delay its happening.

The Aesir gods had also learned that their foretold doom at Ragnarok was to happen by the hands of Loki and three of his children. This compelled them to take preventive steps against those that would bring about their doom.

One of their preventative steps was to bind and prevent Loki's children from being able to rise up against them. The three children of Loki in question were: the great wolf Fenrir, the serpent Jörmungandr, and the female Hel.

The gods cast the great serpent Jörmungandr into the deep sea that lies around the lands of Midgard. The serpent grew so large that he was able to encircle Midgard and grasp his own tail. This is how he earned the name as the "Midgard Serpent," for his eventual encirculating it.

The gods then sought to bind the great wolf, Fenrir. Their first two attempts to bind Fenrir failed, as the great wolf easily broke the tethers they tried to use to bind him.

The gods began to fear that they wouldn't be able to bind Fenrir,so Freyr sent his vassal Skírnir as a messenger down into the land of Svartálfaheimr to request that the dwarves that dwelt in that realm would make them a fetter that would be strong enough to tether Fenrir. The dwarves constructed the fetter called Gleipnir which they'd made from six mythical ingredients. The fetter was smooth and soft as a silken ribbon, but strong and firm.

It was only on the third attempt that the god Tyr was successfully able to bind him when he wagered Fenrir that he wouldn't be able to break this tether as he had the previous ones. Fenrir didn't trust that the gods would let him go if they tethered him and he failed to break the fetter, so he refused to let him tether him again.

131

So as a sign of trust, Tyr placed his right hand in Fenrir's mouth as a pledge that if he failed to break the fetter, that Tyr would untether and free him.

Týr with his hand in Fenrir's mouth.[91]

The great wolf Fenrir agreed to allow Tyr to tether him with his other hand. However after Tyr put the tether on he refused to let Fenrir go when he wasn't able to break it, so Fenrir bit Tyr's hand off and devoured it. This is how Tyr became known as the one-handed god.

Odin then cast Loki's daughter Hel to Niflheim and bestowed upon her authority over the nine worlds, in that she must administer board and lodging to those sent to her. Her realm was to take in those whom have died of sickness or old age.

Having taken steps to prevent Loki's children from rising up against them, the gods now felt a false sense of security. That is, until the god Baldr began having dreams

132

about his own death. This worried his mother, Frigg, whom then went around the world and made everything in the world give oaths to never harm her son Baldr.

The gods became so confident in this, that they'd amuse themselves by throwing weapons (or anything else they could find) at him to watch them harmlessly bounce off him. Nothing they threw at him would harm him and they were convinced of Baldr's invincibility. They were convinced that his invincibility would prevent Ragnarok from happening.

Loki was the trickster of the gods and while amused over Baldr's invincibility, asked his mother Frigg if she'd overlooked anything in the World when she sought out oaths from all things to never harm him. Frigg stated that she didn't bother seeking an oath from mistletoe, because she felt it was too small and rather harmless.

Armed with this information, Loki set off to make a spear (sometimes told as an arrow) from mistletoe. He then convinced the blind god, Hod, to throw it at Baldr for amusement to watch it bounce off of him. Hod threw the spear (or fired the arrow), not knowing what it was made of nor that it would do any harm to Baldr, and pierced Baldr with the mistletoe weapon. The mistletoe weapon killed Baldr.

When Baldr died, he went to the Underworld into the realm of the goddess Hel. The Aesir gods were in anguish and decided to send one of them to the underworld (Helheim) to plead to Hel for the release of Baldr.

Hermod, one of Odin's sons, set to make the journey

down the World Tree, Yggdrasil while riding Odin's steed Sleipnir until he reached its roots at the bottom where Hel's realm was located.

Hermod pleading for Baldr's life to the goddess Hel in her realm Hel.[86]

Hermod pleaded on behalf of the Aesir gods for the goddess Hel to release Baldur, but she said she would only release him if they proved that he was as beloved as they claimed he was if the everything in the World wept for him.

Everything in the World did weep for Baldr, except one, the giantess Þökk (possibly Loki in disguise).

Þökk's refusal to weep for Baldr was enough to make the goddess Hel refuse to release him from death until the coming of Ragnarok.

The death of Baldr was a major sign of the coming of Ragnarok and forced the gods to believe in the Völva's prophesy. All they could do now was to begin preparing for it. Any god that had any doubts about Ragnarok's inevitable coming had now long lost any uncertainty.

Loki was punished by using the internal organs of his son, Narfi, to bind him on top of three stones in three places. The lashings tethering Loki turned to iron once they were in place.

Thor's wife, Skaði then placed a poisonous snake over him that continuously dripped venom onto his face. Loki's wife Sigyn tried to collect the venom in a bucket to prevent it from dripping on him, but she had to empty it periodically. When she had to empty the bucket, the dripping venom caused Loki so much pain that when the poison dripped on his face, the pain made him convulse so violently that they resulted in earthquakes. Loki was to be miserably bound this way until the onset of Ragnarök.

Odin spent a great deal of time and energy to select the dead that fell in battle. He sought to make sure he had the strongest and bravest to fight with him in the coming battle of Ragnarok. These fallen warriors called Einherjar were brought to the Halls of Valhalla by the Valkyries. Odin collected these Einherjar and built his great army while watching for more signs of the coming of Ragnarok.

There will be three roosters that warn all of the coming of Ragnarok by their crowing:

- The crimson rooster called Fjalar will crow in the forest of Jotunheim to warn the Jötnar (frost giants) living in Gálgviðr.

- The golden rooster named Gullinkambi will crow to Valhalla to warn the Æsir gods.

- The third, a soot-red rooster will crow in the halls of the underworld (Helheim) of Hel to warn the dead.

The decay of humanity is another sign of the coming of Ragnarok. In the realm of humans, Midgard (Miðgarðr), people will lose faith in the gods and begin to abandon their traditional ways. They will break oaths, disregard kinship bonds, and fall into having a general nihilistic outlook on everything. Humans will become absent of any moral values, having no real value in anything or its outcome. They will lose faith that anything in their world now or will there ever be, has any meaning or value to it.

Upon the approach of Ragnarok, there will be a Great Winter called, Fimbulwinter (Fimbulvetr). This is the winter of all winters that will last three years without any summers in between the seasons. The Sun will become useless and will not warm anything. Snow will fall from every direction and freeze everything.

All of mankind will begin to die off from the cold, except two humans that will survive named Líf and Lifthrasir (Lífþrasir). They will be safely hid in the

Yggdrasil tree (also referred to as being called "Hoddmímis holt").

An illustration of Lífthrasir and Líf.[93]

It was during this time that the wolf sons of the Great wolf, Fenrir will succeed in their never ending quest of trying to devour the Sun and the Moon. Sköll, the wolf that's been chasing the Sun every day, will finally catch the Sun and devour it. His wolf brother Hati, who chased the

Moon will also finally catch the Moon and devours it.

When the Sun and Moon are devoured, the stars will fall from the sky and the Earth will tremble with the trees becoming uprooted and mountains crumbling. This great trembling causes all binds around Loki to break as well.

Loki is set free and immediately heads to the realm of Hel to collect all the dead in Helheim for battle. The great wolf Fenrir will also break loose from the bond that was placed on him by the Aesir gods when he bit off Tyr's hand.

Fenrir, now free and vengeful, will then charge forward with his mouth agape with the bottom of his mouth touching the Earth and the top touching the sky. He will devour everything in his path while his eyes and nostrils spray flames everywhere.

His brother, Jörmungandr, the Great Midgard serpent will ferociously come out of the sea, causing great tidal waves and he will spit venom into the sky and sea.

While this is all happening, the sky will split in two and from the realm of fire, the sons of Muspell (demons and fire giants) will ride forth. They will be led by Surtr whom will be surrounded by flames and be wielding his flaming sword that shines brighter than the Sun.

They will be joined by the great wolf Fenrir, the great serpent Jörmungandr, and all the frost giants (jötnar). Loki will be sailing a ship made from human finger and toe nails called, "Naglfar." The ship will be filled with the dead from Hel's realm and together they will join the others and come to the field of Vígríðr to do battle with the Aesir gods.

Heimdall, the watchman and guardian of Valhalla, will see them coming and sound his great horn Gjallarhorn, warning the gods of the invasion.

The giants will set upon destroying the god's realm and the cosmos along with it. The Aesir gods will move to battle them.

Odin is then swallowed whole by the great wolf Fenrir. Tyr moves to battle the great wolf and also falls to Fenrir. Odin's son Víðarr will step forward and avenge his father's death by tearing Fenrir's jaws apart and killing the great wolf by stabbing it in the heart with his spear.

Thor will meet his nemesis the serpent Jörmungandr in combat and furiously fight the great serpent to the death. Thor will defeat the beast, but Thor dies as well, collapsing after taking just nine steps. Not only do Thor and the sea serpent Jormungand kill each other,

The Aesir god Greyr fights Surtr and falls to the jötunn's flaming sword. Freyr then battles Surtr and they slay each other in close combat.

Surtr and Freyr slay each other.[94]

Heimdall and Loki kill each other while in battle as well. Many of the gods and giants fall in battle as the flames spread by Surtr burn and devour everything as the ravaged worlds crumble and sink back into the sea and vanish completely below the waves.

Once the flames caused by Surtr have been completely sated, the perfect darkness and silence of the great void Ginnungagap will reign again once more.

The Earth will then re-emerge from the sea and the land becomes more lush and fruitful than it had ever been since it was created the previous time.

Baldr will return from the underworld and the surviving gods, such as the Odin's sons Víðarr and Váli will live in the new temples of the gods and Thor's sons Móði and Magni will possess Thor's hammer Mjolnir.

The two surviving humans, Líf and Lífþrasir, that were hidden and surviving off the morning dew, will emerge and repopulate the Earth. And that concludes the event of Ragnarok, when the World is destroyed and recreated.

Chapter 6 – Christianization of the Norse

The Christianization of the Norse took place between the 8th and the 12th centuries. It was a gradual process that took considerable effort by Christians. Christian clergy attempts to convert the Norse proved to be difficult. The Norse people were quite content with their own gods and simply did not wish to be converted. In many cases, conversion was only achieved by force.

Prior to Christianization, the traditional religion of the Norse people was firmly in place. The Norse religion wasn't just a form of worship, it was a part of their culture and way of life. A belief system that was so deeply rooted that it made the concept of the original sin and other Christian beliefs just too hard for the Norse people to understand or believe.

Because of hard core Norse beliefs, converting the Norse was a task that took Christendom a relatively long time to achieve. As far as the Norse were concerned, their gods had brought them nothing but success in battle and they had absolutely no reason to embrace the Christian god.

This led to the Christians to seek Norse conversion by

any and all means possible, including converting existing Norse beliefs, practices, and cultural beliefs into Christian ideology. This was often practiced in order to introduce Christian beliefs in a way that the Norse could relate to in comparison to the gods they already knew well.

So to help convert the Norse to Christian ways, many pre-existing Norse practices and customs were converted into Christian practices, such as the Christening of a child for example. The missionaries adopted the name-fastening ceremony practiced by the Norse pagans and adopted it into their own religious ceremony know today as a christening ceremony.

When a child was born, there was a great deal of ceremony conducted by the Norse. For example, a newly born infant would be placed on the ground and then remained there until he or she was picked up by their father (or next of kin in his absence) and placed in the folds of his cloak. This act of picking up the infant by the father ceremoniously acknowledged the legitimacy and acceptance by the father as his offspring.

The father then examined the infant for any abnormalities and judged whether or not it had a future. This process decided the fate of the child as to whether it was to live or be left exposed to the wilderness to die. A custom commonly known to be practiced by the Greek Spartans.

If the child was free of defects and deemed to live, a sacred religious rite called the *Ausa Vatni* was preformed. This ceremony was conducted by either sprinkling or pouring water over the child and then naming the child.

This ceremony was an ancient sacred rite of the Old Norse religion that predates Christian baptism. To expose a child after this ceremony was preformed was considered murder. The rite of Ausa Vatri was also practiced by some of the Northern Frankish tribes. Some forms of Christian baptism are based on this rite and only changed it in name by early Christian missionaries whom made it a part of Christian practice.

There is also record of the sacred rite being practiced in the Norse Sagas. One example is the birth of Sigurd, whom was the son of Ragnar Lothbrok. Ragnar's wife, Kráka (also known as Aslaug) bore Ragnar a son and they carried the child to Ragnar to see him. Ragnar took the boy and placed him in his cloak and gave him the name Sigurd. In addition, it was customary to give a gift to the child during the naming ceremony. In the Saga of Ragnar Lothbrok, it is said he took a gold ring and gave it to his son as a "name-fastening (Old Norse 'nafnfesti')."

The gift given to a child during the nafnfesti (name-fastening) rite varied from either rings, weapons, and other tokens, to even such things as entitlement to farms, or lands.

In addition to the *Ausa Vatni* rite and *Nafnfesti* ceremony of giving a gift while naming the child, it was also customary practice to give a child a gift when they cut their first tooth. This practice later evolved into modern day's practice of the "tooth fairy."

Another well known ancient Norse practice worth

mentioning that was taken into Christian practice was the celebration of Yule. The pagan holiday of "Yuletide" became what we in the modern day know as Christmas. The Scandinavians still use the word "Jul" or "Yule" for Christmas. This celebration was originally a fertility rite used to ensure good harvests in the following seasons. The Old Norse practice of receiving a blessing from spirit of the farm that guarded and protected it was later substituted by receiving blessings from a Christian priest.

However before Christianization, each Norse farm was believed to have its own land spirit or protector which the modern Danes and Norwegians call a "Nisse" ("Tomte" in Swedish). The Nisse spirit was replaced with the Christian St. Nicholas or Santa Claus. However, the conversion attempt wasn't completely successful by the Christian missionaries and to this day on Christmas Eve many children in Scandinavia whom aren't waiting for Father Christmas, instead await a Nisse or Tomte to arrive with gifts.

Once the Norse had a better understanding of Christian concepts as they were compared to their own established religion, they eventually were able to accept Christianity and its beliefs. Many early successful conversions of the Norse was done by relating Christian concepts as closely to Norse practices as possible.

However, most conversion attempts were done by means of entire communities converting as a whole rather than individual conversions. Mass conversions were carried out by methods such as demanding conversions through subjugation. The subjects of a leader would be forced to convert.

Typically, the Norse leader or King would convert to Christianity and as an opportunity to solidify their power, they would force all their subjects to convert as well. Peace treaties formed with other Christian monarchs were often only achieved if the Viking leader converted to Christianity and had their men do so as well. Even when at the Norse's mercy and being demanded silver payments to release cities conquered by Norse raiders (Vikings). They managed to buy the Norse off with caches of silver and an agreement of Christian conversion.

So instead of trying to convert individuals to become Christians, the community would be ordered to convert by their leader. This made the clergy's job easy as entire regions would become converted by order of their King.

Not all agreements went as planned for Christian monarchs and clergy when they ordered their followers to convert. There were instances, such as when Jarl Haakon was in Denmark. Harald Bluetooth forced him to accept being baptized as a Christian and to take clergymen with him to Norway in order to spread Christianity in Norway. Haakon had no choice by to accept, but when favorable winds allowed Haakon to set sail and leave, he commanded the clergymen off his boats to return ashore as he and his men left.

Haakon ordering the clergymen off his boats.[38]

Once an area was ordered by their leader to convert, missionaries, priests, and monks would then come in to finish the process. Once the people were converted, the old gods and practices would be outlawed. Entire communities would be baptized and swear oaths to forsake the old gods and take in Christ as their only god.

Further subjugation took place through instruction and discipleship training by christian missionaries that would be set up. Even still, foreign missionaries did get resistance, often for no other reason than distrust of them simply because they were foreigners.

The English missionaries were more successful in their attempts at spreading Christianity because most of them came from England. It was as simple as that. English missionaries were more trusted because they were from conquered areas that were under subjugation by the Norse.

The Norse had already gotten used to the English people and their customs. The Norse weren't as suspicious of the English missionaries, militarily or politically, as they were the missionaries from other Norse lands, such as the Germanic Kingdoms or Francia.

One attraction to Christianity was that Norse pagans were impressed and tempted by the sheer materialistic power of world of Christendom. Christian lands, especially to the south, were rich with bountiful crops. This led many Norse to believe that the Christian god was more caring and generous.

Their pagan beliefs and faiths were mostly focused by gaining material prosperity through specific gods that gave attention to specific things. For example, they worshiped gods of agriculture because they wanted their crops to grow. Please the gods that favored cattle so that they would produce more milk. The Norse gods weren't particularly concerned with the human plight and were very hard to please.

When these Norse pagans looked at the wealth and power coming out of Christian Europe, they were impressed. Obviously the Christian God would deliver the goods and gave greater concern towards humankind. The Christians built bigger buildings and formed wealthy cities. Christians possessed more and it was of greater beauty and quality. The Christian crops were bountiful, so it was obvious to the Norse that the Christian god was more generous.

This was why when the Norse did begin converting,

some pagans had no problem converting to Christianity. They had the hope that conversion would give them material prosperity that was nonexistent with their current gods. The Norse gods didn't seem to care about them, but perhaps the Christian god will.

However, a majority of Norse converts would often continue with their pagan practices. Norse paganism was also a part of their culture and was very hard to simply cast aside. But thankfully for the Norse, strict Christianity wasn't enforced. Besides, the Norse were polytheistic and had many gods, accepting a new god alongside their already many existing gods wasn't that hard for them to do or accept. They didn't exactly convert to a new god and discard the old ones, they simply added another one to the count.

Polytheist pagans have lots and lots of gods. Gods for everything: gods of weather, of harvest, of the sea, of the sky, of beer making, of battle, and so forth. The Christian god was simply another god to them. The concept of a monotheistic faith of having only one god didn't sink in very well at first. This is why even after being converted, it took a very long period for Christians to wash away the Norse belief in many gods, goddesses, spirits, fairies, elves and giants from coexisting with faith in Christ.

The image of a "Victorious Christ" frequently appears in early Germanic and Norse art, suggesting that Christian missionaries presented Christ to the Norse as a figure of strength and as a victor in battle. Using the Book of Revelation that tells of Christ's victory over Satan to play a central part in the spread of Christianity among the Vikings, whom looked to Odin and Thor for such attributes.

Even still, completely converting the Norse to true monotheistic Christianity was an extremely difficult task. The Norse never had anything against the Christians or their religious beliefs. The notorious Viking attacks on monasteries were due to the fact that they were rich and poorly defended. These raids were nothing more than opportunities for a Viking raid and had nothing to do with the Christian religion itself. The Christian monasteries were easy pickings.

Many Norse monks didn't take the whole religious life all that seriously. Becoming a monk at the time was seen more as a means of acquiring an education and learning to read and write. The strict conversions did not take place until later, especially when the age of Protestantism was sweeping across Europe.

For the most part, Christian conversions weren't taken seriously at all by the Norse. Missionary monks that came into Norse areas trying to convert them simply were ignored and tolerated because they were regarded as peaceful and harmless.

The first serious conversion attempts began somewhere between 710 AD and 718 AD, when a Anglo-Saxon monk named Willibrord had made unsuccessful attempts to convert the Danes. This took place during the reign of King Ongendus (also known as King Angantyr). Unfortunately, his efforts to spread the Christian faith were simply not appealing to the Norse Danes.

Not one to give up, in 725 AD, Willibrord made another attempt and led another mission to Denmark in hopes of conversions. Yet even though he was well received by the king, his mission once again had little effect on the general populace.

This failure did not stop the missionary monks from trying, as they were usually sent and backed by the Frankish King (Holy Roman Emperor) Charlemagne and other rulers in the Kingdoms bordering south of the Norse. Church missions were strategically built where they could make attempts to convert the populace.

However, even after a church was established they were sometimes later targeted by pagans. In the Netherlands, a church in Deventer was sacked and burned by a Saxon expedition in January of 772 AD. This act gave the Frankish King Charlemagne the justification (Casus belli) to wage war on the Saxons.

The war began with the Franks invading Saxon territory. They conquered and subjugated the Engrians and destroyed the sacred symbol "Irminsul" at Eresburg (near Paderborn, Germany). The Sacred Symbol "Irminsul" represented "Yggdrasil," the pillar tree that supported the skies and cosmos and was considered sacred to Odin and the gods. Which made it extremely sacred to the Norse. Its destruction was a grave insult to the Norse.

The destruction of Irminsul by King Charlemagne.[40]

When the King of the Franks, Charlemagne, chopped down the Irminsûl, the sacred column or holy tree of the Saxons, it began the Viking Age and relentless raids on Frankish lands. The retaliation was ruthless. In a series of several ambushes, Charlemagne had also assassinated around 5,000 Saxon nobility and effectively decimated the Saxon's ability to further resist his armies any longer. This allowed further subjugation and forced conversions into Christianity of the Saxon Norse.

Unfortunate for the Saxons, the methodology used by King Charlemagne was to convert his enemies by essentially defeating and killing them. After they were dead, he'd have a priest say some words in Latin and sprinkle some water over them and thus they were converted as Christians.

These were the events that influenced the Norse in Scandinavia to finally cease all hostilities against each other and focus their attention on a mutual hatred and thus began to wage war and attacks on Christianity. This was part of what started what we know as the Viking Age, as anything Christian was considered by Norsemen as a legitimate and justified target to raid.

Prior to this event in 772 AD, the kings of Norway were at war and allied against the Danes with Charlemagne. However, when the Frankish King had the Irminsûl cut down and the Saxon Nobles assassinated, the various kings of Norway switched sides, uniting with their Norse brethren (the Danes) and went to war against Charlemagne.

This effectively put a damper on any attempts by missionaries with their efforts to convert the Norse into Christianity.

It was later, after Charlemagne, in the 820's AD and onward that the missionary Ansgar and his followers, with the support of the new Frankish King, Louis the Pious were able to establish missions in both Denmark and Sweden. Even though the missions were made with the support local Norse rulers, once again the missionaries had made little to no influence on the population as a whole.

The missionary Ansgar converting the Norse.[39]

It was in 826 AD, that Harald Klak, the King of Jutland, was forced to flee Denmark by the Danish King Horik I. King Harald was forced to go to King Louis I of Germany and seek his help in getting back his lands in Jutland. King Louis I offered to make Harald Duke of Frisia if he would give up the old Norse gods and convert to Christianity. Harald agreed to this proposal. He, his family, and the 400 Danes that were with him were all then baptized as Christians.

When Harald returned to Jutland, the missionary monk Ansgar was assigned to accompany him and oversee Christian adherence among the new Norse converts. It was when King Horik I once again forced Harald Klak from Denmark that the monk Ansgar left Denmark and focused his efforts in Sweden instead. In 829 AD, Ansgar established a small Christian community in Birka, on the island of Björkö in Sweden. By 831 AD, the Archdiocese of Hamburg was founded and assigned the proselytizing responsibility for converting the Scandinavians from their traditional Nordic beliefs to Christianity.

Regardless of the mass conversions spreading through Scandinavia, Sweden did face a pagan reaction in the mid-11th century and Christianity did not become firmly established there until in the 12th century.

The greater increasing numbers of converts was because from the 11th to the 14th century, Christian society in Europe became less tolerant of other religions and beliefs. This was the time period when the Christian hammer slammed down on pagans and heretics. This is also when we see the persecution of Jews and the crusades against Muslims happening. At this time, forcible conversion became widely accepted, especially in Scandinavia and the Baltics, the only European region that remained resistant and unconverted.

When the Protestant Reformation began, it spread through Scandinavia like a wildfire. Protestantism took hold easier that did the earlier Catholic Church's attempts.

All of Scandinavia had ultimately adopted Lutheranism over the course of the 16th century, because the monarchs of Denmark (whom also ruled Norway and Iceland) and Sweden (whom also ruled Finland) converted to that faith and required their subjects to convert as well. The Scandinavian having a firmer grip on their subjects than ever before, had an easier time converting their people from Catholicism to Protestantism.

In Sweden, the Protestant Reformation was spearheaded by Gustav Vasa, whom was elected King of Sweden in 1523 AD. Swedish national conversion to the Protestant faith led to the discontinuance of any official connection between Sweden and the Papacy. Four years later, in 1527 AD, the King of Sweden succeeded in forcing his dominance over the national church. This was when the king took possession over all church property and church appointments required royal approval. The national church and clergy were now subject to civil law, along with Lutheran Protestant ideas and views which were now to be taught in the schools and churches.

Under the reign of King Frederick I in 1523 to 1533 AD, Denmark remained officially Roman Catholic. King Frederick initially persecuted the Lutheran Protestants, but later he began protecting the Lutheran reformers. Due to this religious tolerance of Protestantism, conversions to Lutheranism grew significantly among the Danish population.

King Frederick's son, Christian, was openly Lutheran. When King Frederick died, his Lutheran son was prevented from succession of the throne because of the Catholic hold still in place in the nation. It was when the National Assembly terminated the authority of the Roman Catholic Church in 1536 AD and after his victory in the "Count's War" the following year that he was crowned as King Christian III of Denmark and Norway. At this point he was able to continue the reformation of the state's church and began to enforce Lutheranism in his kingdom. The resistance to this religious change nearly escalated to the point of civil war.

It was also during this time of the Protestant Reformation that Iceland had also adopted Lutheranism in place of its earlier established Roman Catholic religion. However, the Protestant Reformation in Iceland proved to be much more violent than in most of the other lands ruled by Denmark. Iceland had to be converted by force.

It wasn't until Lutheranism was firmly in place that Catholicism was outlawed by Icelandic law. It was outlawed to the point that for more than three centuries no Catholic priest was permitted to even set foot on Iceland.

Chapter 7 – Norse Language

The language used by the Norse people was *'Old Norse'* It was the primary language used in settlements up onto the 14th century when the language eventually developed into the modern North Germanic languages.

The transition period of this language transformation is approximate, because *Old Norse* was still found in written form well into the 15th Century. This was eventually phased out by the church, whom preferred Latin text when writing.

Primitive Norse, or *Ancient Norse* (also called Proto-Norse) was the language of the Scandinavian people prior to the first centuries AD. *Ancient Norse* developed into the characteristic northern Proto-Germanic dialect that attests to the Elder-Futhark inscriptions from the 3rd and 4th centuries. During the Iron Age *Ancient Norse* eventually evolved into the *Old Norse* language used at the beginning of the Viking Age during the 8th Century.

There were three distinct dialects of Old Norse: *Old East Norse*, *Old West Norse*, and *Old Gutnish*.

The *Old Icelandic* language was essentially identical to

Old Norwegian used. Together, the Old Icelandic and Norwegian formed into the *Old West Norse* dialect. This dialect was spoken in the Norse settlements of: Ireland, Scotland, the Isle of Man, and in the Norwegian settlements of Normandy.

The *Old East* dialect of the Norse language was spoken in Denmark, Sweden, and spread as far as to settlements located in Russia. Many Norse followed the Volga river and reached the Black Sea and Caspian Sea to open up trade with Easterners.

This Old Norse dialect used by the Danes was also used in England and in the Danish settlements that were located in Normandy. Gotland and various other settlements in the East spoke the *Old Gutnish* dialect of Norse.

Due to Norse expansion and trade, *Old Norse* was the most widely spoken language in Europe in the 11th century. The Norse language influence ranged all the way to Vinland and Greenland in the West to the Volga River in Russia to the East (which lasted well into the 13th century there).

This map shows the range of Old Norse dialects used in Viking settlements. The language spread the most near coastlines and rivers where Norse built trade settlements and ports. Many reaching further into the country mainland as settlements grew and expanded.

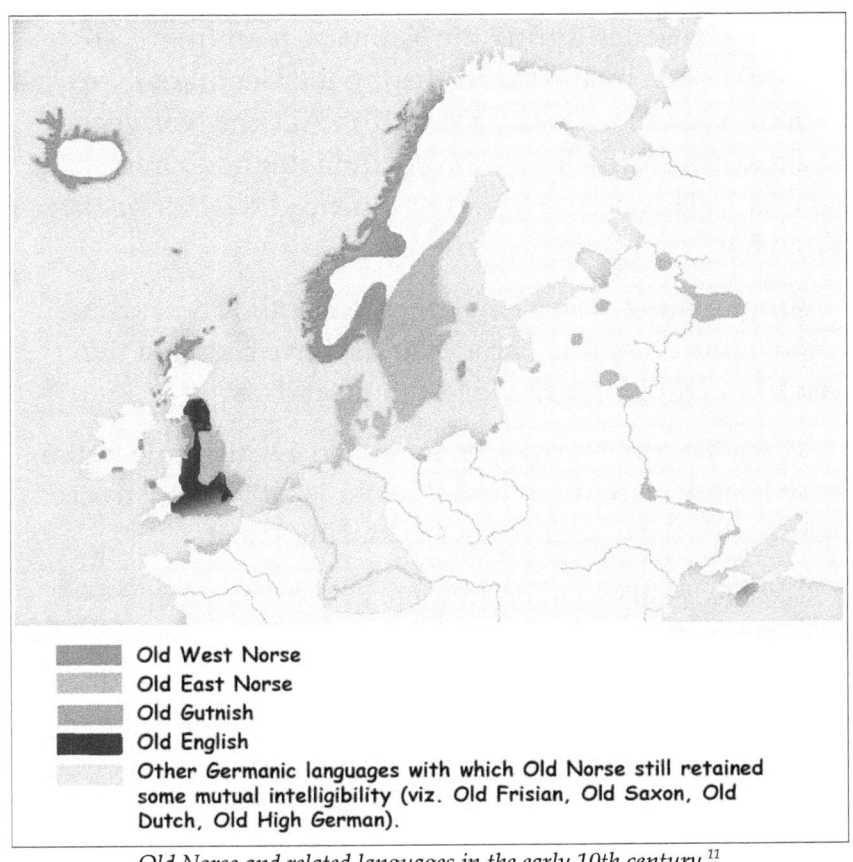

Old West Norse
Old East Norse
Old Gutnish
Old English
Other Germanic languages with which Old Norse still retained some mutual intelligibility (viz. Old Frisian, Old Saxon, Old Dutch, Old High German).

Old Norse and related languages in the early 10th century.[11]

The modern descendants of the Old West Norse dialects spoken today are: Icelandic, Faroese, Norwegian. There are also the now extinct Norn language that was used in the Orkney and the Shetland Islands.

The Danish and Swedish languages are the modern descendants of the Old East Norse dialect. Even though Norwegian is descended from Old West Norse, it has been heavily influenced by Old East Norse Dialect used by the

Danes and Swedes during the Kalmar Union from 1397 to 1523 AD. Then by the Danes during the Denmark–Norway union in 1524 AD. From 1536 to 1814 AD, the Norwegian kingdom was formally dissolved and integrated into Denmark. This period heavily influenced the Norwegian Language.

Among these Norse languages, Icelandic and Faroese (spoken mostly on the Faroe Islands) have changed the least from Old Norse in the last thousand years.

Much like the Norwegian language, Danish rule in the Faroe Islands had influenced the Old West Norse Faroese dialect with the Old East Norse Danish dialect.

Old Norse also had an influence on the English language and that of the Lowland Scots, both of which contain many Old Norse loanwords. Old English and Old Norse are closely related, which is why it shouldn't be of any surprise to an English speaker that Old Norse words look and often sound familiar.

Here are a few examples Old Norse words carried over in English:

they (þæiʀ), their (þæiʀa), them (þæim), flat (flatr), happy (happ), ill (illr), likely (líklígʀ), anger (angr), bag (baggi), bait (bæit), band (band), egg (ægg), gap (gap), husband (húsbóndi), cake (kaka), kid (kið), knife (knífʀ), leg (læggʀ), sale (sala), scrap (skrap), seat (sæti), sister (systir), skin (skinn), skirt (skyrta), sky (ský), slaughter (slátr), snare (snara), steak (stæik), are (er), blend (blanda), call (kalla), cast (kasta), get (geta), give (gifa/gefa), hit (hitta), lift (lyfta), raise (ræisa), take (taka), want (vanta).

Note the Norse use of the letter "*thorn*" or "þorn" (Þ, þ). This sound carried over into use in the Old English, Gothic, and Icelandic alphabets, as well as some dialects of Middle English. It is still used today by Icelandic speakers.

Thorn(þ) is sometimes still used in writing to give it a "Medieval" or "Olde English" feel to it. Most often, this example is used in business signs and logos.

Th eventually replaced the written *Thorn*(þ) sound, especially in writing. *Thorn*(þ) is replaced by th in several words, such as: the (þe), they (þæiʀ), their (þæiʀa), that (þetta) and them (þæim).

Thorn (Þ) is often mistaken as being a **Y** by modern English speakers. For example, the **Þ** in *Þe Olde English* is commonly mistaken as being: *Ye Olde English*.

The letter thorn þ is most easily mistaken when written in Middle English as *Winn* Ƿ. The Middle English *Winn* Ƿ has a greater chance of being mistaken as being a Y.

It's easy to see how "Ƿe Olde Tavern (**The** Olde Tavern)" can be mistaken as "**Y**e Olde Tavern."

The picture below displays comparison examples of the letter thorn being hand written and how easily it is mistaken as a Y.

Capital Thorn   Lower case

Þ   þ

Other variations that make it look
like a "Y"

An example from an old written text.

A business sign in England, whereas it
gets mistaken as a "Y". The sign reads,
"The Olde Chippy" not "Ye Olde Chippy."

Examples of Thorn þ where it is mistaken as a "Y."

Old Norse also influenced the development of the
Norman language. Many of the Norse settlements that
eventually founded Normandy were mostly either Dane or
Norwegian and heavily influenced the language used.

There are also a number of other languages, while not
closely related, that have also been heavily influenced by
Old Norse: the Norman dialects, Scottish Gaelic, Waterford
Irish, Russian, Belarrusian, Lithuanian, Finnish, German, all
the Scandinavian languages, and Estonian as a few
examples.

The language influence stretches over an area that covers the northern half of Europe in general. Most of these languages have a number of Old Norse loanwords just as the English language does.

The Icelandic language is the closest to original Old Norse that was spoken by the Vikings. In fact, because modern written Icelandic comes from the Old Norse phonemic writing system; Icelandic-speakers can read Old Norse, only varying slightly in spelling, semantics, and word order. However, this is only written Icelandic, as in verbal Icelandic pronunciation the vowel phonemes have changed as much as in the other Northern Germanic languages used today influenced by Old Norse.

Written Norse is called the **Futhark**, more commonly known as the **Runic Alphabet**. The Norse Runic Alphabet is said by the Ancient Norse to have been given to them by god Odin himself.

Odin had learned *the Runic Alphabet* after hanging himself upside down from the Yggsdrasil tree and then pierced himself with a spear. He peered below into the shadowy depths below for nine days at the edge between life and death until the Runes revealed themselves to him. It is said, they not only showed him their forms but their secret meanings. Odin was a seeker of knowledge and wisdom, whom even sacrificed one of his eyes for wisdom.

The **Elder Futhark** (Runic Alphabet) is named after the initial phoneme of the first six runes: F, U, Th, A, R and K, The Elder Futhark consists of twenty-four runes, which are arranged in three groups of eight runes called ætts.

This graphic shows the Elder Futhark Runic Alphabet.

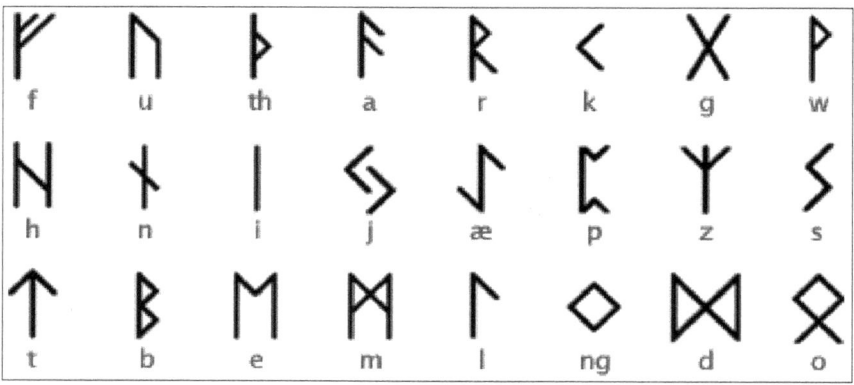

The Elder Futhark

It is generally agreed among scholars that the Runic Alphabet originated sometime in the 1st century AD. Some estimates place it about the 1st Century BC.

The Norse Runic Alphabet had somewhat altered in around the 9th Century AD in Scandinavia into what's called the **Younger Futhark.** The Alphabet was reduced to only 16 characters from the Elder Futhark's original 24. This is probably because of language changes made from Proto-Norse (Ancient Norse) into the Old Norse that was used from the 8th to 12th Centuries.

However, use of the Runic Alphabet had drastically declined in the 12th Century. After the Christianization of Scandinavia, most writing was done using the Latin Alphabet favored by the Roman Catholic Church.

But before then during the Viking Age it was the Younger Futhark Alphabet that was used predominately by the Norse and was known as the "Alphabet of the Norsemen" in Europe.

The Younger Futhark Alphabet divided into two branches: The Swedish/Norwegian Short twig and the Danish long branch. There is debate as to why there are differences. One argument claims that the Danish long branch was used for inscription purposes, such as stone inscriptions for records and that the Swedish/Norwegian short twig was for inscribes on wood for private or official messages in everyday use.

This graphic comparison shows the differences in the Danish long branch and the Norwegian short twig with their Latin letter equivalents.

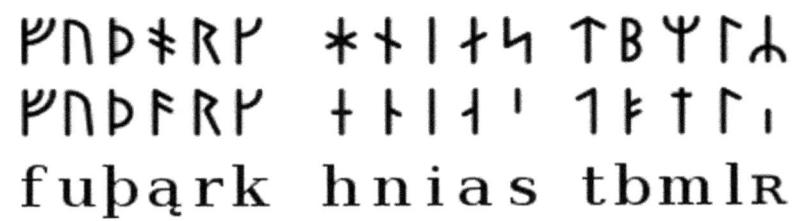

The Younger Futhark: Danish long branch (top), Swedish/Norwegian short twig (middle) and Latin letters (bottom).

Runic characters survived in marginal use after the Christianization of Scandinavia in the form of the **Hälsinge Runes (Staveless Runes)** used in the 10th through the 12th centuries. The *Staveless Runes* seem to be a simplification of the Swedish/Norwegian short twig runic alphabet, being that they are staveless and are lacking vertical strokes.

Although staveless, the alphabet retains the staves of the Younger Futhark runes.

Here is an graphic example of the Staveless Runes or Hälsinge Runes.

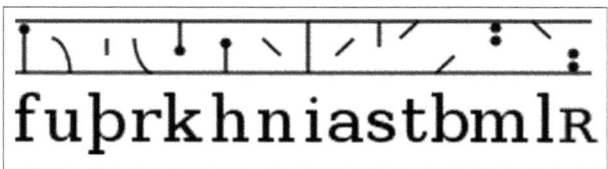

Hälsinge runes (staveless runes).

During the Middles Ages use of the Younger Futhark had expanded along with the expansion of the Norse. The language was becoming more complex and writing more in common use, the Runic Alphabet evolved into the **Medieval Runes (Futhork)** Alphabet during the end of the Viking age in the 11th century and becoming fully formed by the 13th century.

This graphic compares Medieval Runes, or what is known as Futhork, and their Latin alphabet translations.

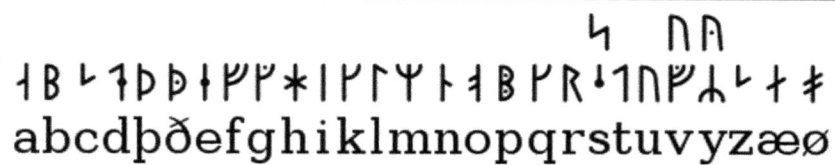

Medieval Runes

Most probably, the Medieval Runes had evolved with the competition of the Latin Alphabet which was fast expanding with the Christianization of Europe and Scandinavia. The Latin Alphabet could be copied into Norse easier with this expanded Medieval Rune (Futhork) alphabet.

By the 13th Century, the Runic Alphabet had mostly fallen out of use in favor the Latin alphabet, except still being in use by artisans, farmers, and traders whom continued to use it to communicate and mark items. As the use of Latin became the standard for writing throughout Europe and Scandinavia, Runic writing was rarely used. A few hundred years later, the use of the Runic Alphabet became almost extinct and nearly forgotten.

Chapter 8 – Norse Life

Daily life for the Norse was not much different from that of anyone else. Notably, they did live a slightly tougher life given the more rugged terrain and weather experienced in the North. But adaptation to the climate and terrain was the key to successful survival. The Norse were innovative and made the best out of what they had. Their way of life reflected these traits and evolved over time as needed.

During the Viking era, most Norse families lived on a farm in a longhouse. A longhouse was a large, hall-like building that sometimes were up to 30 meters long. Longhouses were built with walls made from timber or stone and a thick turf roofs to retain heat. In the center of the typical Norse longhouse was the hearth, providing warmth and light for the occupants inside.

Originally, longhouses were just large single room halls, housing members of the family, farm workers (the thralls) and even the livestock together under the same great roof. It was later that the longhouse became divided, having several separate rooms which would usually include bedrooms and kitchen area. A longhouse was the typical setup for those living on farms.

Those living in the towns and settlements had houses that generally were either made of wood or made of wattle and daub (a lattice of wooden stakes covered with sand and clay) type of construction.

Typical of living in most towns or settlements, the houses were built closer together. Although houses built in town were smaller, they still had enough room for their own rubbish pit, yards and a workshop. The workshop was important, as living in town generally meant you were an artisan or smith of some form.

Cleanliness was important to the Norse. Contrary to the dirty image of a savage and barbaric people the Vikings tend to be portrayed as in film, archaeological evidence proves that this as a myth and false stereotype.

Perhaps the most telling comment about Norse cleanliness comes from the English cleric, John of Wallingford. The cleric John had bitterly complained about the Viking men of the Danelaw because they combed their hair, took a bath on Saturday, and changed their woolen garments frequently.

He claimed that they performed these unchristian and heathen acts in an attempt to seduce high-born English women.[12] He blamed their habit of bathing, combing their hair daily, and because they regularly laundered and changed their clothes, that they were able to undermine the virtue of married women and even seduce the daughters of nobles.[13]

Besides being clean, the Norse also wore well made clothing. The typical Viking or Norse person was usually dressed in garments made from wool. Typically during the Viking Age, most textiles were made of worsted wool in twill patterns. These wools were carefully woven, supple, and were attractively textured and often dyed in bright colors.

Having a decent weaver in the extended family was a necessity if one wanted to be smartly dressed. Another necessity for the well dressed individual was jewelry. A typical decorative ornament and symbol of status worn by many Viking men was an armring.

In Viking times, armrings or béag were given by powerful lords to secure allegiance from their followers. Bestowing such gifts was a demonstration of wealth and power by Viking lords and were worn with pride by those that followed them. These armbands were also symbols of coming of age, when a boy became a young man and swore an oath of loyalty to his lord. They were not only seen as a token of manhood, but as acceptance by their lord and peers.

10th Century Wendover Arm-Ring (British Museum).

Both Norse men and women took great pride in their appearance, and besides the armring worn by men to show their allegiance, both women and men also wore a variety of ornately bejeweled gold and silver brooches, rings and necklaces. Ornate combs were also one of the most common artifacts that are uncovered by archaeologists at Scandinavian settlements.

Personal hygiene items are some of the most common finds. The Norse were a very clean people. Not only were many types of combs found, but also such things as ear spoons.

Another common stereotype of the "Viking" is one of them all having blonde or red braided hair. It is true that the Norse favored light colored hair. Ahmad ibn Fadlan, an Arabic emissary that had contact with the Norsemen of the Rus Tribe, noted that the Norsemen would bleach their beards to a saffron yellow color.

Although it is not documented, it is most probable that they bleached their hair as well. The Norse bleached their hair using a predominately basic soap mixture they made from goat fat and beech wood ashes which had excess lye in it that caused the bleaching action.

The Roman, Gaius Plinius Secundus (better known as Pliny the Elder) also mentioned the Norse practice of bleaching their hair among the Germanic tribes he had contact with. He also pointed out that he felt that the men were more likely than women to bleach their hair.

Hair styles among the Norse varied according to an individual's preference and needs. Usually only thralls (slaves) wore their hair very short, a hair style that marked their status as a thrall.

However contrary to the long braided hair depicted of the Viking warrior, the average Norseman wore his hair about collar or shoulder length. An individual's beard was kept as long as was comfortable for him. In fact, a Viking warrior might make their choices of hairstyle based on minimizing the hazard of having their hair or beard grabbed in combat. Combat was an extremely violent confrontation and any means to win a fight were used, even grabbing hair or articles of clothing to bring your opponent down.

Clothing choices for combat differed than those of everyday wear. We know of the different kinds of armor worn by Viking warriors, but seldom is it ever mentioned about what they wore on a daily basis. This is because actual artifacts of Norse clothing of the Viking era are hard to find. The reason being is because cloth and fabric tend to decay quickly over time, but there have been a few items of Viking era clothing found.

In York, named Jorvik during the Viking Age, boots and shoes have been discovered made of calfskin or goatskin. But even these finds were decayed, making it hard to tell exactly what the Norse people wore during the Viking Age. So to fill in the gaps, we must rely upon poems and artwork of the time to piece it all together. From these poetic and artful depictions. We know that Norse women wore either woolen or linen smocks that were fastened with brooches and pleated underdresses.

The smock layer actually differed in cut and design from one archeological site to another and from one time period to another. For example in the 9ᵗʰ century, the Norwegians wore a unpleated smock that was cut in a wide oval or "boat" neckline in the tunic fashion.

In Denmark during the 10ᵗʰ century, the Danes wore a unpleated smock that was refined with set-in sleeves, shoulder seams, and gores. In Brika Sweden, they wore long sleeved pleated smock underdress that was made from a lightweight undyed linen during the 10ᵗʰ century.

These underdresses were often covered by another full length tunic-like gown with long sleeves and then there was an apron dress pinned over that.

Much care was put into these full length gowns. On the sleeves and torso of the outer layer gown (and often the apron dress over it) they would have had elegant ornamentation in the form of embroidery, appliqué, silk trimming, and tablet-woven bands.

The apron dress worn over the outer smock or gown is often called a "Viking apron." This garment was not a typical apron as worn today when cooking, but a complete over garment, so the descriptive name "apron-dress" is more befitting for this garment.

The Viking style apron-dress was worn over the shoulders and secured in place by a pair of brooches that were hooked through narrow loop straps. In addition to the gowns and apron dresses worn over them, married Norse women also wore scarves on their heads.

Reconstruction of the Køstrup apron-dress.[14]

During the Viking era, men worn woolen tunics over trouser type leg coverings. There were at least two types of leg coverings: a wide, knee-length, baggy type and a narrow, fitted full-length type of trouser.

Several finds of trousers dating to the Migration Era at around 400 to 800 AD tell us that the narrow full length types of trouser were worn by the Norse way back then. A site at Thorsbjerg Mose in Denmark, trousers found more or less intact, had the sophisticated Migration Era that required three separate pieces cut for the crotch gusset alone.

These trouser finds alone disprove any claims made that early period garments worn by the Norse were simple and untailored. The leggings of the Migration Era Thorsbjerg trousers even extended into foot coverings, just like children's pajamas.

The remains of a pair of trousers found in Birka, Sweden were probably of the short and baggy style. These trousers were made from linen and had little metal eyes set into their lower edges. The accompanying leg stockings were made from wool with little hooks sewn on to them. The woolen leg stockings were hooked to the lower edges of the linen trousers just below the knees.

The little hooks used to connect the trousers to the leg stockings were called "garter hooks." Even the Vikings had issues with their socks falling down.

Along with trousers, Norse men wore an under tunic and smock. During the Migration Era, a jarl at Evebø Norway wore two tunics, one over the other. He wore a knee-length red wool undertunic that was trimmed at the neck, wrists, and finished edge hems. His undertunic also had complex wool tablet-weaving patterns with various depictions of beasts in yellow, red, and black. The under-tunic's cuffs were secured with bronze wrist clasps, a feature fairly common in period.

The smocks discovered that were worn at the Danish-Northern Germanic Norse settlement at Hedeby were of two basic types. Both types have a rounded neckline with rounded armholes for set-in sleeves and had separate front and back panels sewn together at the shoulders. However, they differed in their side-seams: one type had narrow, slit sides, while the other type was wider with inserted gores for fullness at the hems.

Most were made from wool and some were even dyed. The sleeves on the smocks were tapered at the lower arm, so at the wrists they fit fairly snugly and they could also be cut in more than one piece to achieve a more complicated taper.

Some of the smocks from the Birka, Sweden area had keyhole style necklines rather than Danish rounded ones. The front and back panels were cut in one piece and weren't sewn together with shoulder seams.

On top of the tunics worn, the Norse wore an over-tunic. An over-tunic at Evebø, Norway belonging to a jarl was dyed blue, made of wool and was decorated at the neck with tablet-woven wool bands patterned with animals in two colors. The over-tunic also had silver clasps, however it's unknown whether they were cuff clasps or clasps for the front of the over-tunic.

It is most probable that the clasps fastened in the front on the chest like a coat. However, the over-tunics were not coats, as they had actual coats that were worn on the outer layer as weather demanded.

There were two basic coat layer types during the Viking Era that were most commonly used by the Norse. Basically not much different than today, there was the "jacket" and the "coat." The jacket was lighter and wrapped around without a fastening device, while the coat was heavier and buttoned securely closed.

Viking era jackets have been found in several spots in the Norse-dominated world and appear to have been a very old tradition.

We have a good idea of coat styles from a helmet that was found at the "Sutton Hoo" ship burial site. It had human figures depicted on it whom were dressed in what look like bathrobes or large coats. This depicted coat consisted of a short tunic open all down the front with diagonal, overlapping flaps.

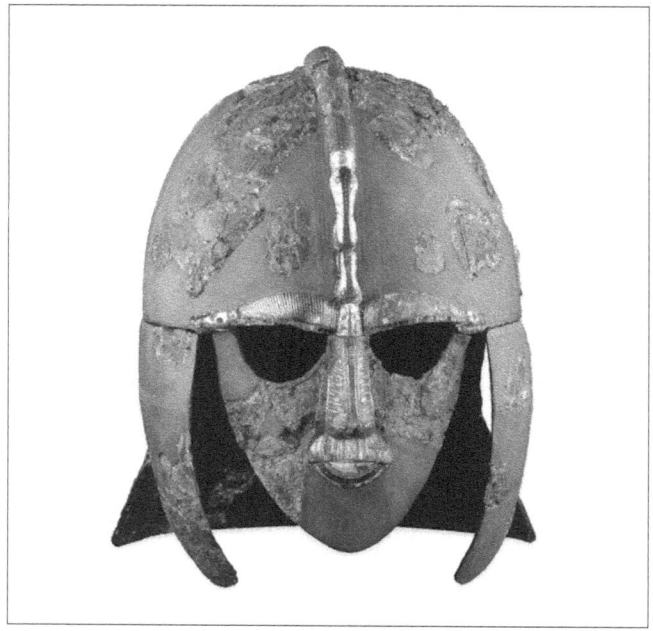

The Sutton Hoo helmet.[95]

Saxon graves in parts of England and Europe also have a coat layer of this design type that were ornamented on the lapel and down the front with gold-brocaded tablet weaving.

Fragments of a jacket found at the Hedeby trading site were made of plain 2/2 twill. Although incomplete, the jacket is believed to have been hip-length and trimmed with fake fur made of wool along the hem and down the front edges.

A type of Norse coat known as the "caftan" or "Rus riding coat" may have been an explicitly eastern Norse concept of the Swedes and Viking Rus tribes during the 9th and 10th centuries. This type of coat was a long over-garment that buttoned from neck to the waistline and was decorated with specialized and elaborate metal trimmings.

There have been five remains of these kinds of overcoats found and each of them had a row of cast metal shank-buttons. Several other coats have been identified which had the right sort of elaborate trimmings, but hadn't the associated buttons. Nevertheless, this does not mean that they didn't have buttons or other kinds of fasteners, because organic items such as wood or bone buttons disintegrate over time and leave little or no trace in a burial site. So it's very likely that these coats had buttons, even though none were found at the sites.

The Norse also wore cloaks and caps in the wintertime. The basic Viking cloak was rectangular cloak and was fastened with a cloak pin.

Cloak pins were usually of the pennannular brooch type or ring-headed pin types. Cloaks came in a variety of weights and weaves that ranged from lightweight patterned twills to the "rogvarfelðr" types that were heavy cloaks napped with "fake-fur" made from wool.

A cloak found in Evebø, Norway was an elaborate lightweight rectangular cloak that had fringed edges. It was red plaid with blue and yellow stripes in a 12x12cm repeat. At the edges of the cloak were tablet-woven bands of either blue or green with beasts in either yellow or red.

At a site in Jorvik (York), Fragments of red and undyed tufted wool have been found. Remnants of a heavy cloak with blue and red pile loops as long as a thumb have been found in Birka, Sweden.

Burial sites at Birka, Sweden have included cloaks worn on the body in the grave or were deposited near the body. These cloaks worn were usually thick, heavy blue ones that were either pinned at the shoulder or the hip. Several burial sites included a cloak that was deposited near the body. There were five men's burial sites that dated to the 9th century and all had cloak pins at the shoulder. Several cloaks from the 10th century were found pinned at the hip rather than the shoulder.

The Norse also wore a variety of woolen hats, caps, and other head wear. Some partially silken peaked hats with and without metal buttons have been found as well. Hats were worn for fashion as well as functionally such as keeping one's head warm and dry.

Belts rarely survive time and generally deteriorate, leaving little to no evidence. Although a variety of belt buckles have been found in many sites, most of them are simple in design. Shoes and boots, also made of leather that deteriorates, are also difficult and rare finds. However, some examples have been found.

The shoes found dating to the Viking Era were either made with separate soles that were stitched to the leather uppers or were "hide" shoes that had the upper and sole cut in one piece and then stitched to itself.

Most shoes types found were either half-boots or ankle shoes. There were some shoes that were slip-ons, while some were tied with leather lacing, and some that used lappets with cylindrical leather buttons. The materials and leather most often used for making shoes, were usually goat hide, deerskin, calf, sheep, and cowhide.

A Viking Male – reconstruction.[15]

We know that life for the Norse was hard considering their climate. Their struggle led them to expanding their culture to reaches further than most any of the cultures in the world. We normally depict them as a hard working, hard fighting people whom were masters in trade and innovation.

But all work and no play makes Thorvald a dull and bored Viking.

As with other cultures, the Norse people not only worked hard but also set aside time for leisure activities. Most leisure that we know about were in the forms of celebrations whereas they held feasts celebrating successful raids, trade expeditions, and marriages. This is in addition to holidays and community Thing meetings.

Norse banquets, there would be a variety of meats served including beef, pork, lamb, fish and other seafoods, wild game, and goat. A variety of other foods as well, such as breads that consisted of various seeds that gave it flavor. And most notably the Norse people drank large quantities of wine, beer, and mead.

Life was well blended with a combination of leisure and labor.

Consistently practiced were the craft skills which played an important part in Norse society. Skilled weavers made woolen cloth which was not only used for clothing, but also for the sails on the masts of their ships. Smithing was a well known skill of the Norse, whom not only created items of metal but were able to repair their weapons or farming tools as needed.

A variety of craftsmen made items that were carved with ornate figures and patterns. Musical instruments have also been excavated from Norse settlements such as flutes and panpipes.

The typical Norse life was filled with music and as much pleasure as it was filled with the daily drudges of life's daily struggles.

Chapter 9 – Norse Trade

For as long as history can trace, the Norse have been well known as great traders. Their trade reach extended all the way to the Far East, through Russia and the Black Sea, to the Middle East. Regular trade thrived throughout Europe and in the Mediterranean. The Volga trade route along the Volga River connected Norse tradesmen all the way to the southern shores of the Caspian Sea to trade with Muslim countries, sometimes as far as Baghdad through the Euphrates and Tigris Rivers trade routes. The reach of the Norse was extensive.

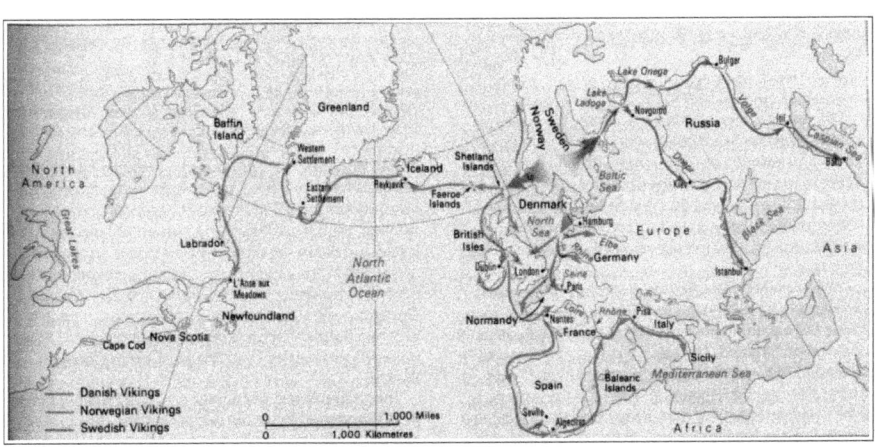

Map showing the reach of Norse trade.

Norse trade settlements were everywhere and even some scholars argue that during the Viking Age if many Norse traders were mislabeled in history as being marauding Viking raiders rather than the welcomed peaceful traders that most of them were.

In fact a great many modern cities throughout England, Scotland, Ireland, and across Europe actually began as welcomed peaceful Norse trading settlements, rather than the result of conquered entities. Skilled craftsmen and smiths were drawn to and even relocated to these trade centers as well.

The Norse had established regular ports and settlements where trade was held for the bartering of wares peacefully without any fear of molestation. Booths were built in these places so that native and foreign merchants alike could come and trade goods such as: furs, dried meats, skins, garments, grain, slaves, weapons, metals, and just about everything and anything. Götland was regarded as a major trade center for the North.

The trade ships heading to trade ports were free from Viking attacks, as plundering merchant vessels seems to have been considered unmanly. The Vikings, although having a reputation for raiding targets of opportunity, were not pirates.

Kaup-skip (trade ships), unlike the longships and other war vessels, were easily recognized as being ships of trade. Kaup-skips didn't have shields on the sides or war pennants and dragon ornaments of the war ships. The Viking longships stuck out as raiders or obvious vessels of war, whereas the knarrs and other merchant ships were obvious.

St. Olaf mentions trade ships having red and white striped sails to clearly identify them as peaceful trade vessels.

Replica Merchant Knarr with red and white striped sail marking it a trader ship.[9ε]

Traders (Kaufman) were respected and trading considered as a high calling. Even the sons of kings became famous warriors, seafarers, and traders.

Kings made trade agreements with traders and controlled some trade to an extent, such as domestic grain which was forbidden to be exported during hard years. Incentive was always made to keep traders coming and importing goods they couldn't get otherwise. This also allowed exportation of local goods, which opened the door for profit and taxes.

The Norse had a greater value for silver than they did for gold as far as trade standards were considered. The Norse used a monetary standard of what is called a 'Bang.' A *'Bang'* was a spiral ring of silver that was used for trade before the regular presence of silver coins as a standard.

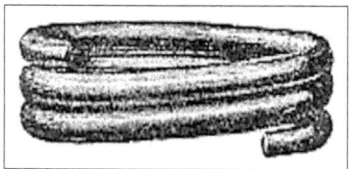

Drawing of a Norse "Bang" (ring).

The Bang values were measured by marks and aurar. One mark equaled eight aurar (1 oz.), one eyrir (singular for aurar) equaled eight ortugar, and one ortug (singular for ortugar) equaled ten (or sixty) penningar (singular penning, German: pfenning).

It was customary to weigh the medium of exchange by scales. With all things being equal, trust was a limited commodity. Even when the bang fell out of use, the new silver coin standards were weighed by scale to verify their weights when used in trading.

Chapter 10 – Norse Law and Government

The Norse had a class structure to their society. They had kings, priests, jarls and lords, freemen and slaves (thralls). Before the formal organization of the Scandinavian countries, the Norse were considered as a single people consisting of various family clans. Nordic society was set and organized with a deliberate means to the ends.

Norse social stratification was layered like most other cultures of the World. The Kings and royal families were at the very top of the class structure. Kings were generally placed and chosen by birth, as being the heirs to current kings in power over petty kingdoms.

Next down the social layer were the **Jarls**, whom were the chiefs of the clans. The united family clans were ruled by Jarls until the end of the Viking Age when the separate Scandinavian nations emerged and became ruled by centralized kings. The Jarls were the chieftain landowners and warrior noblemen that pretty much controlled everything within their realms.

In the middle of the social layer cake were the **Karls**,

these were some of the freemen that owned large farms and owned slaves (thralls). Some of the Karls (freemen) worked as fishermen, craftsmen or boat builders as well. The typical Norseman was a Karl or freeman. At the coming of age, a young Karl will usually pledge their allegiance to the local Jarl and receive an arm band.

The lowest on the social layer were the **thralls** (slaves), whom were considered as property and were often traded for large amounts of silver and gold. In most cases, about the value of a cow. In Norse terminology, "thralls" were male slaves and "ambátt" was the term for a female slave.

The mark of a thrall was to have closely cropped hair and they were to wear a white vadmal or kulf (coat) to distinguish themselves from freemen. Thralls and ambátts generally wore used clothing and clothes made from undyed cheap cloth. Colorful garments and embroidery was generally reserved for free Norse and nobility. The best to those whom could afford it.

War captives from expeditions were the chief supply for slaves and they came from places such as: the European mainland, mostly from the various Frankish Kingdoms, Britain, Ireland, Scotland, Spain, and even from the various shores along the Mediterranean. Thralls were acquired from everywhere, the Norse did not discriminate.

However, thralldom wasn't a permanent placement in life if one could help it. Sometimes a thrall would be fortunate enough to be able to buy their freedom from their master. Those whom belonged to wealthy masters were often allowed to work for themselves and eventually be

196

able to acquire the means to buy their own freedom.

It was more commonplace for a slave to buy their freedom from their masters than to be set or made free. They either paid the full sum and became a freeman at once or paid part of the sum down and the rest owed by working off the debt for their master as an indentured servant. Freedmen enslaved by debt, so to speak.

Norse Law

Law and order is a necessity among all civilized people in order to peacefully live amongst each other. The Norse, like all other people, made their own laws to uphold peace and justice between them. At a gathering, they made their laws and passed their judgments on the law breakers at an assembly called the **Thing**.

The Thing (þing) was a public assembly of which all freemen would have a say in the governance of the land and people. The old Norse clans formed the Thing as a balancing structure for the leaders and freemen of the country to meet at least once a year, or as needed to settle matters.

The gathering of karls and jarls at the Thing dealt with electing or recognizing other jarls, clan leaders, or even kings. It was at the Thing meetings they made and enacted laws. This was also when they made judgments following the law before a law-speaker. A law-speaker was someone whom memorized and recited the law to ensure it was followed.

The thing, although not consistent, held much of the same laws throughout the Norse world and weren't written but memorized by the Law-Speaker. It wasn't until the Christianization of the Norse was when the laws began to be written down.

A Thing assembly typically met in each region for a week during the Spring and Autumn. From around 902 AD onward in Iceland, of which there wasn't a king or centralized ruler, they held a meeting called an **Althing**.

The Norse Althing is considered to be Northern Europe's first national assembly, much like the centralized assemblies held by the Roman Senate in the Southern portion of Europe. However, unlike the Romans whom only gave voice to the members of the Senate, the Norse Althing gave voice to all freeman.

The mutually agreed recognized powers bestowed to the Thing allowed it to set taxes, decide and confirm who was king and even argue and negotiate property disputes and marital affairs. It was also at the Thing that murders and other crimes were investigated.

An accused murderer might call upon the support of twelve men to swear his or her innocence, similar to what we consider a jury today. If the assembled freemen at the Thing meeting found the accused person to be guilty of murder, then the guilty person might be required to pay a fine (weregild) to the victim's family.

The concept of "Weregild" was a system of value that was placed on all humans and property. This was usually the value paid to affected families or owners of lost or damaged property. This is similar to a modern civil lawsuit today when a victim or a victim's family sues for monetary damages.

Sometimes a murderer would be found guilty and sentenced to death, or be banished and outlawed from the country for a set period of time (as was found with Erik the Red). The relatives of the victim could also demand that the wrongdoing be settled with a duel to the death, called a Holmgang.

Germanic Thing depicted by Marcus Aurelius (AD 193)[16]

Although the assembly of a Thing was often dominated by those with the most power and influence within the clans, such as chieftain jarls, kings, and the wealthy. The purpose of the Thing was to maintain universally recognized laws and try to give an equal voice amongst the people.

The very existence of the Thing was necessary to prevent social disorder and tribal feuds. Not an easy task as it was customary with the Norse that every member of a clan was obligated to avenge the injuries against its dead and mutilated. The Thing assembly prevented wars by allowing disputes to be peacefully heard and the demand for reparations be settled by means other than outright blood feuds between clans.

There were various levels of Thing assemblies, starting from the smaller local Things to the larger high leveled Althings where the local Things would be represented. Much like a representative congress or parliament, at the Althing a representative of the clan would attend and speak on behalf of their clan before the other clan representatives.

The location of a Thing assembly was often held at a religious site or other well known trade location. They were held at locations that were well known or near landmarks of the day so they could be found by distant members.

The Thing eventually evolved into Parliaments and still reflects the original concept that the Norse had for a representative government. The 'Storting' (Great Thing) is the name of the Norwegian Parliament. The Swedish speaking people of Finland are represented by the 'Folkting' ('Folks Thing' or Thing of the People) and the Sami are represented by the Sameting ('Sami Thing' or Thing of the Sami).

Disputes settled by Holmgang.

Not everything could be settled by talks and negotiation. This is when justice demanded the blood of another. A **Holmgang** was a duel and a commonly recognized way to settle disputes by the Norse. The word "holmgang" translates to "Island Walk" which refers to a hide or cloak which was about three meters long on each side that was staked to the ground of which was the boundaries that the participants had to stay in during the duel.

Egill Skallagrímsson engaging in holmgang with Berg-Önundr.[17]

Just like a duel, regardless of social status, a person could be challenged to settle a dispute by means of the Holmgang. The duel usually took place within three to seven days after the challenge and if one didn't show up, then the other was considered the winner of the dispute by default.

If it was the challenger of the holmgang that didn't show up, then they would be outlawed and labeled as a 'niðingr' (a coward that had no honor and was beneath everyone else – the lowest of low).

In some cases, a capable warrior could stand in behalf of a clearly outclassed participant of a holmgang. A person's more capable son or someone from their clan to champion on their behalf.

The results of a holmgang was not considered murder and thus a weregild was not required to be paid by the victor, even though it was seen in the film "The 13th Warrior," the victor of a dual had paid weregild after winning a duel.

Chapter 11 – Norse Warfare

The Roman Tactius wrote his observations on Germanic and Norse warfare practices. He made his observations from a gathering of collected tribes that were a mix of Germanic tribesmen and the Norse that had joined them. They had gathered to face the Roman Legions and Tactius made note of their methods and weaponry.

He wrote that he could tell by their weapons that iron wasn't plentiful. During their time of conflict with the Romans, that swords or broad lances were seldom used and that they generally carried a spear. Tactius noted that their spears had an iron blade that was short and narrow, but so sharp and manageable that they employed them either in close or distant fighting.

A spear and a shield were all the armor of their cavalry as well. Each man in the infantry had several missile weapons that they hurled at an immense distance. The warriors were either naked or lightly covered with a small mantle. There was no uniformity amongst the warriors and their shields were the only things decorated with the choicest of colors.

Few warriors were equipped with a coat of chain mail, and scarcely here and there was an individual wearing a helmet.

Their horses were not remarkable, having neither beauty nor swiftness and they were not trained in various formations as those practiced by the Romans. The cavalry either charged straight forward or wheeled once to the right in compact formations so that none of them were left behind.

Their principal strength relied on their infantry and in engagement would be intermixed with their cavalry. The agility of the foot soldiers proved that they were accustomed with the nature of equestrian combat. The most agile selected of their youth from the whole body and placed in the front of the lines.

Their battle lines were set up in wedge formations (boar formations). When they gave ground, as a prudent strategy rather than cowardice, they rallied and reformed. Fear was nonexistent in their ranks.

The greatest disgrace that can befall them is to abandon their shields and run from battle. A person branded with cowardice is neither permitted to join in religious rites nor enter assemblies. A coward after having escaped from battle is put an end by hanging.

Generals and warband leaders commanded less through the force of authority than by their own examples of valor. If a leader is daring, adventurous, and stood out in action, then they procured obedience by the admiration of the men they inspired.

Obedience in battle was not an act of military discipline, but by the instigation of the god whom they believed to be present with warriors and watching them. They even carried certain images and standards taken from their sacred groves that represented their gods with them to the battlefield.

Tactius pointed out that their squadrons and battalions are not formed by men haphazardly collected, but by the assemblage of families and clans. One of the principal incentives to a warrior's courage is that they keep their families within hearing distance. This was particularly true with the Norse that came down to aid the Germanic tribes united. The incentive of victory was promised lands to resettle. For the Norse warriors that brought their families with nowhere else to go, it was victory or death.

The yells of their women and the cries of their children keep them brave and are also the most revered witnesses of each man's conduct in the face of the enemy. The women offer encouragement to those whom are fighting and will even bring them food. To prevent the men from wavering in combat, the women rallied them by crying out as to what would happen to them and their children if they fail, such as being slain or enslaved by their opponents. This forced the warriors to fight even more ferociously, fighting to the death.

These women also tended to the relief of men's wounds with neither dread to the number of wounds nor searching out the gashes. They carried off their slain even while the battle remained undecided.

Norse Battle Tactics

The Norse had no formal standing army nor were they drilled in maneuver like the Roman Soldiers were. They did not fight in regular battle formations and weapons training started when they were youths as a regular part of life. The Norse were a warrior and ax culture. War was apart of their regular life and aspiring warriors would normally be armed by their lords or be rewarded by weapons by their lords. Lords waged war frequently to maintain a following and to maintain power against rivals.

A standard formation universally taught in preparation for battle was that young warriors would line up and interlock their shields to form a shield wall for protection. Typically a veteran warrior would have the younger inexperienced men form a shield wall on either side of them as they directed them in battle.

The leaders would have a special bodyguard, either hurscarls, ulfhednar, or berserkers. These were men consisting of their best veteran warriors that would stand behind the younger warriors and give support, direction, and encouragement.

In medieval Scandinavia the armies were formed by means of the 'leidang' (leiðangr in Old Norse). The leidang was a levy of free farmers that were conscripted into coastal fleets for seasonal excursions and in defense of the king or jarl's realm. The name 'fryd' was used by Germanic invaders and later. The fyrd were the conscripted men that filled the ranks of a local militia in which all freemen had to serve. The Anglo-Saxon army's ranks were the able-bodied men called into action within the realm of a king or jarl. Those whom refused military service were probably executed for cowardice, but the laws claimed that they would be subject to fines or loss of their land. The ability to buy one's way out of going to battle hugely depended upon one's ability to pay such a sum.

The battle was usually began by throwing a spear over the enemy s line which was dedicated to Odin and then this was followed by a shower of spears, arrows, and a variety of other assorted missiles at the enemy line.

After a thorough missile barrage, the Norse would then try to break through and rout the opposition off the battlefield, which included trying to capture or kill the opposition's leader.

One of the battle formations that Norse warriors formed to break through the enemy's lines was called the **"svinfylking" (boar formation)**. The svinfylking was a battle formation where a group of heavily armed warriors (usually 20 to 30) would interlock their shields to form a wedge that had the center pointing towards the enemy's formation. The triangular wedge tapered back on each side from the center point to make a tight spearhead.

The Viking warriors would get in a "boar formation" wedge and then charge forward in this tight interlocked formation, spearheading into the enemy's line and breaking through by sheer force alone. Much like a boar's charge.

The sheer force of this charge was tenacious enough that the wedge would punch a hole right through the opposing force's shield wall or line formation. Spearheading through the enemy's formation in this "boar formation" would spread panic in the enemy and break their lines, turning the battle in favor for the Norseman. Several boar wedge formations could also be grouped side by side forming a zigzag line pattern against the enemy's line and break through their ranks.

Use of the "svinfylking" (boar formation) was unique to the Norse and early Germanic people at the time, as the Romans did not document this as a tactic used by the Saxons or any other culture they had come against.

The successful use of a formation of this type most probably required training and considerable practice. It was probably taught and practiced enroute to the battlefield by experienced warriors with irregular troops, as most called up Norse armies were levied (conscripted) and were usually farmers by trade. Although it is also likely to have been learned earlier, as most Norse men were taught and practiced the use of weapons and tactics from boyhood.

Often the Boar formation not only consisted of warriors interlocked to form the wedge, but would have archers inside the formation behind the warriors on the front line protecting them. They would fire arrows and throw spears at the enemy as the formation bashed its way through.

The Svinfylking formation also would usually thwart

cavalry charges on it because the horses and riders would be pushed aside from the wedge's center point and then attacked by the outer wedge's warriors with spears causing complete chaos among the cavalry's horses.

The Svinfylking formation's basic weakness was being flanked by the enemy, because the formation were based on its frontal point by sheer forward force. Additionally, if the boar formation didn't immediately break the enemy line from its forward wedged charge, then the men in the formation wouldn't hold very long and would be forced to break off and reform.

The Norse also formed the standard shield wall formation of the day as well. When in the shield wall, most attacks against your opponent are made overhead. The overhead attack is an attempt to hit over the top of the enemy's shield while aiming at their head and trying to bash or split them in the head, neck, or shoulders. Most thrusts while in a shield wall formation would go against the enemy s shield and open yourself up to similar attacks as you must open a small gap in the wall to allow you to thrust.

Spears are generally used effectively with two hands while thrusting at the enemy chest and waist level. Spears were best used by warriors behind the shield wall that were thrusting and targeting enemy warriors that were involved in another fight. However, this move also exposed a spearman to similar attacks from the opposing side using similar methods. A shield wall was essentially shoved, hacked, and stabbed down by sheer force.

Once the shield wall was broke down, individual fights ensued and were most likely settled by using opportunistic wounding blows that left an opponent disabled but not dead – out of the fight and no longer a threat.

Quite often, legs and arms would be the only exposed targets that would be easy to hit. Obviously the limbs were the most tempting target against a warrior that was wearing a mail shirt or other body armor that would also be protected by their shield. The head was usually crowned with a helmet, so the exposed legs, arms, face and neck would be the best areas to target.

Many of the fallen warriors are usually found with major leg injuries where they were incapacitated and then left behind to bleed to death on the field as the battle went on to be decided. It was a common practice of the day for the victor to return and slay the enemy's wounded that remained.

Beyond special formations and tactics, the Vikings also had special troops that would reap fear into the enemy and instill encouragement on the friendly side. One kind of these special warriors were the infamous **berserkers**.

Berserkers were warriors that would work themselves into a battle frenzy so much that they ignored pain and injury. Often, there would be many berserkers formed into groups and would be set loose on the enemy as shock troops. The berserkers believed that the god Odin would personally protect them from harm and so they often wore no armor into battle.

There is only speculation as to what a berserker really

212

was, as there are no accurate records of them. The word berserk comes from two words, 'ber' meaning bear and 'serk' meaning shirt. This probably means that these battle frenzied super warriors more likely wore bear skin shirts to battle as a symbol of their status.

Another special kind of warrior were the **Úlfhéðinn** (plural **Ulfhednar** or in Old Norse *Úlfhéðnar*), meaning **"wolf's head wearer."** These elite Norse warriors had attributes similar to that of a berserker. These warriors were also sometimes described in Norse Sagas as being special warriors of the god Odin himself.

The Ulfhednar were identifiable by the pelt of a wolf or a wolf's head that they wore on their heads when they went into battle. Just like berserkers, these elite Ulfhednar warriors would whip themselves into a fearsome battle frenzy and were often used as the personal bodyguards of a king or jarl chieftain.

Another special warrior worth mentioning were the **Huscarls** (Húskarlar in Old Norse). They were "household troops" that were often the most experienced and best equipped warriors around. These special warriors were usually of freemen (Old Norse 'Karl' or Old English 'Carl') status whom had sworn loyalty oaths to be professional warriors in the service of a jarl or king, typically as personal bodyguards.

It was normal for them to be placed in the front of battle ranks or used as shock troops. Their presence would bolster the morale of the other warriors as they also gave battle guidance with their experience. They're also used as completely separate units that operated behind the main battle lines and provided an instant reactionary force to the army's flanks or reinforcing areas on the battle line which may be weakening on the front. It fell to the Huscarls the task of defending the battle standard and the army's leader.

With all these tactics and methods of using special shock troops, a Viking Age leader was expected to lead his army from the front. After having achieved the respectable position of leadership by their skillful use of weaponry and battle tactics, a Viking leader was expected to stand in the amidst of a battle, personally leading the charge.

The Norse were a superstitious people and would depend on the leader's personal fortunes and favor of the gods. If the leader fell in battle, it was likely that his army would withdraw or rout from the field, although his personal bodyguard (the huscarls) were expected to stand over him and die with their leader.

It was also normal for the leaders of Viking Age armies to seek each other out on the battlefield and achieve a quick victory by slaying and cutting off the head of the opposing army's leader. Although this tactic wasn't usually successful, there have been several cases where the huscarls of one army would charge and breach the enemy's shield wall and slay the opposing side's leader. This was presumably part of a charge that was led personally by the earl or king. A Viking king or jarl led by example, not by title. If they were not brave and battle worthy, they would not be followed.

Chapter 12 – Norse Armor and Weaponry

So how did the Norse arm themselves? What we know of Norse weaponry and armor is from what we've found predominately in grave sites from the early periods. Additionally, we get information from depictions that were carved on stones, tales in the Sagas, and from legal texts written in the later periods which give us a general idea and paint clues for us to piece together about how Norsemen armed for combat during the Viking Age.

During the time the laws made by the Gulating (Old Norse: Gulaþing) in Norway, Denmark, and Sweden required that every able-bodied man should own weapons according to his status.

In Norway, a sword or ax, spear and shield must be owned and maintained. In Sweden and Denmark, this was a sword, spear, shield and iron helmet that was to be for each man. Additionally, it was common for some laws to required a mail shirt or protective jerkin and a bow and 24 arrows be provided for each bench seat in a ship or that a local chieftain be required to provide these items.

As part of a coming of age ceremony, a Norse freeman

would receive an armring from his lord, pledging his loyalty and service to that lord. That is, a pledge to come to war or raid when that lord called them to. This was a standard practice and a part of Norse culture. Bearing an arm ring was also a status symbol. Some lords would also reward their new subjects awarded arm rings that had sworn oaths to them with weapons. The use of weapons was also apart of life. From an early age, a lad would train in the use of weaponry as a part of everyday life. This was a common practice and custom among the different Norse clans.

So what were these weapons? The Shield, the Ax, and the Spear. Proficiency with the bow was a bonus and a skill most likely already being mastered and in use for hunting.

The Shield

There is Skaldic poetry that is specifically dedicated to shields. They are known as the "shield poems." The shield was as much a part of Norse culture as was the ax. It was well developed and one of the best shields made.

The Viking shield was very different from that of the shields used around the World. The shields were made from wood with a metal center and were colorfully painted. Upon first glance, there doesn't seem to anything special about these shields but you'd be very wrong to think so.

The shield designed by the Norse was a superior and

well thought out concept. It was not made from solid wood as were the other culture's shields of the day. This is in contrast of what you would think you wanted from a shield. Something solid enough to block hits from weapons and arrows. Something durable enough to protect you. Something strong enough to protect you from the swing of a sword, thrust of a spear, or an arrow with your name on it.

The Viking shield was a brilliant concept and ahead of its time. It was actually made from what we would think of as soft and flimsy wood like fir, alder and poplar. Norse shields were not made from heavy oak or other known solid woods. In the Sagas, it is written that they were to be made from 'flexible' woods such as linden, lime, or basswood. Wow, that's a flimsy wood to be making a shield from. Why would the fierce Vikings use such a flimsy wood, instead of hard woods like their opponents?

The Norse chose this flexible wood because, unlike the hard woods such as oak, Viking shields weren't inclined to split so easily upon a successful hard impact. When there was a successful split of the Norse shield by a weapon, the fibers of the wood tended to bind around blade which prevented them from cutting any deeper unless a lot more pressure was applied. Something you definitely didn't want to be wasting your time doing in combat. Hesitating in attempts to finish splitting your opponent's shield gave your opponent the opportunity to split your head open.

Another characteristic about the wood the Norse chose to use for their shields was the fact that instead of bearing the blunt of a solid hit, which would also cause the shield to split or shatter, the 'flimsy' wood of the Viking shield would bounce and absorb some of the impact. This made the shield more effective.

They also reinforced their shields with leather quite frequently and occasionally had iron around the rim for added strength.

The shield wasn't made of a single sheet of wood, but of planks. The shield from the Gokstad ship was about 3 feet in diameter and shows us clearly how the shield planks were laid. The planks were tightly formed running along the grain of the wood. This caused blows against the grain to bounce back, adsorbing the energy and blows along the grain would grip the weapon.

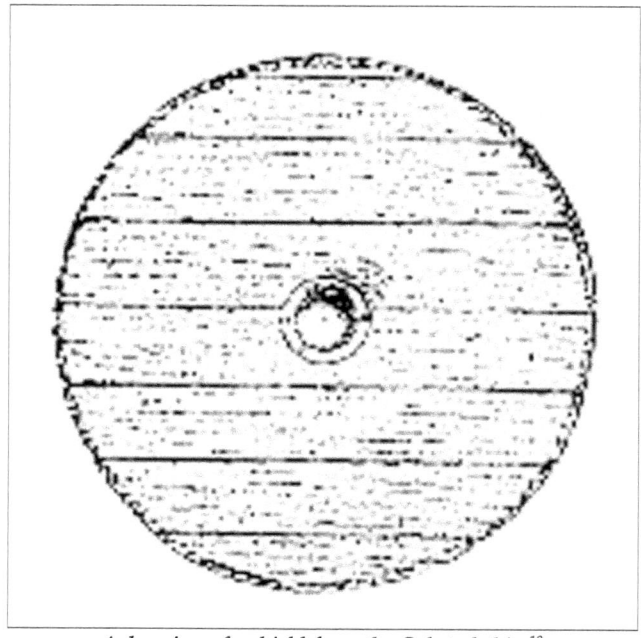

A drawing of a shield from the Gokstad ship.[18]

An addition to the flexibility of the Viking shield that helped repel hits was that it was painted. It wasn't painted for looks or uniformity like the Greek or Roman shields were with identical markings and color to identify them to their lord or unit. The Viking shield was painted specifically for a function other than identification. One thing you'll notice about a Viking shield is that in a band of warriors, they all had different color shields with different markings. Markings that were painted on their shields that had no real significance in relation to marking who they were or who they belonged to.

This was because the Viking shield was painted for a reason that had nothing to do with units or cohorts. It was painted for the sole purpose of hiding the grains of the wood of the shield. If an opponent were able to see the wood grains on a shield, they'd be able to figure out where to hit it in order to split it.

The Viking shield was intentionally painted to conceal the wood grains, it was not painted to look pretty or to mark their loyalties. The cleverness of this was when their opponent went to strike the shield, they had no hint as to the shield's most vulnerable place or where to strike or hit it.

Add the fact that the Norse shield was flexible and would absorb the hits and even would bounce their opponent's weapon back at them. If an attacker did get a lucky hit along the grain of the shield's wood, then their blade would most likely get caught in the wood's fibers and instantly give the shield wielder an advantage over them.

There is one more clever thing about the Viking shield, the center part of it called the shield boss was made of metal. Usually the shield boss was made of iron and was concave with the shield and had a handle inside of it.

The advantage of this was that it was like having a fist made of iron. You could bash the enemy with it and even use it to parry and block blows.

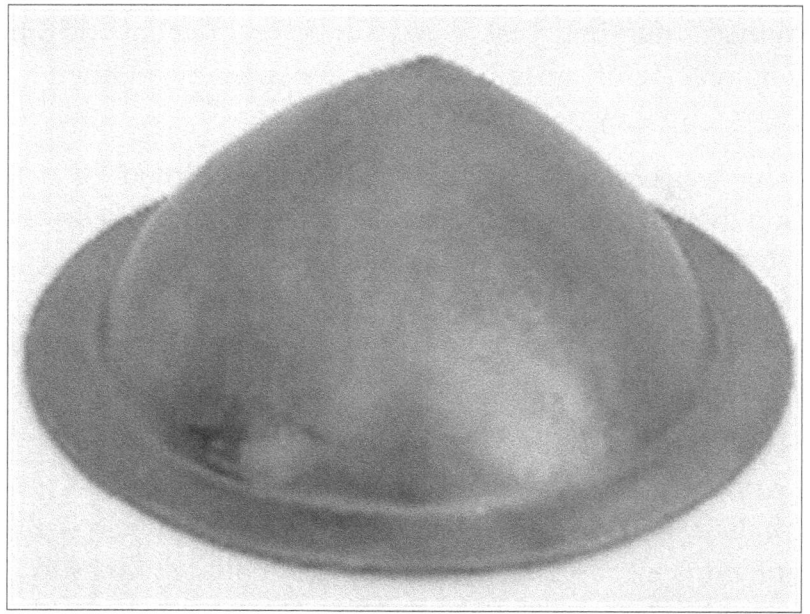

Iron shield boss replica.

The shield center was the primary place where the wielder would use to repel and block strikes against them. The shield boss having a handle made it easier to wield as it fell upon the natural place in the hand and would also serve as an iron fist, so to speak, to strike an opponent with the shield.

222

With the wood being light weight and the handle also being in the center and formed with iron, the shield was easier to wield and use than the shields used by other nations. Other nations such as the Greeks and Romans, strapped their shields to their forearms which made them difficult to wield in melee combat.

Modern replica of a Viking Shield.[19]

Viking shields were also heavily used in defensive and offfensive formations. The skjaldborg (shield fort) was a main defensive formation where Norse warriors would create a line of interlocked shields and thrust their spears at their opponents. And of course, the previously mentioned Norse shield formation called the "svinfylking" (boar formation), where warriors created a wedge formation and charged forward to burst through the enemy's front line or even thwart an enemy calvary advance on them.

The Ax

The ax is probably the most characteristic weapon of the Vikings. One cannot think of the Vikings without thinking about the ax. The Norse evolved into an ax culture during their Stone Age period. Axes of several types have been found in many burial sites, as the ax was not just a weapon but also a tool. It was a common item among the Norse. Axes have even been found in female burial sites. Depictions of the ax are also shown on several carved stones.

The head of the ax was generally formed from wrought iron with its sharpened edge made from steel. It took less skill to forge an ax, so even the poorest of the Norse could afford one. An ax was needed for simple daily life such as wood cutting and splitting. So in a time of need for battle, even a wood ax could be used for battle if the need arose.

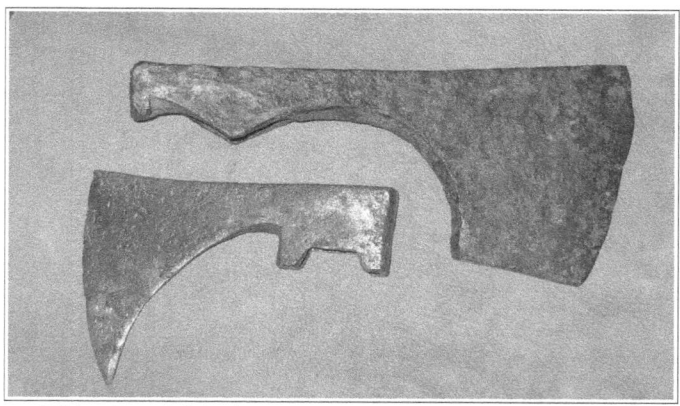

Viking Bearded Ax (top), German Horseman's Ax (bottom).[20]

Axes specifically meant for battle were designed and made differently than those of farm and woodsman axes. Battle axes were designed to cut and smash through a man. Even designed to bash apart shields and split through a helmet. Some battle axes evolved into long handled, two-handed axes that could smash through shield and armor.

Contrary to the fictional stereotype and as cool looking as they are, double headed battle axes were not made by the Norse. Almost all axes forged by the Norse were single bladed.

One of the more popular battle axes was the Dane Ax (Danish Ax). It was an ax that consisted of a wide, thin blade that was 'pronounced' at both the toe and heel of the bit with the toe swept inward for better shearing power.

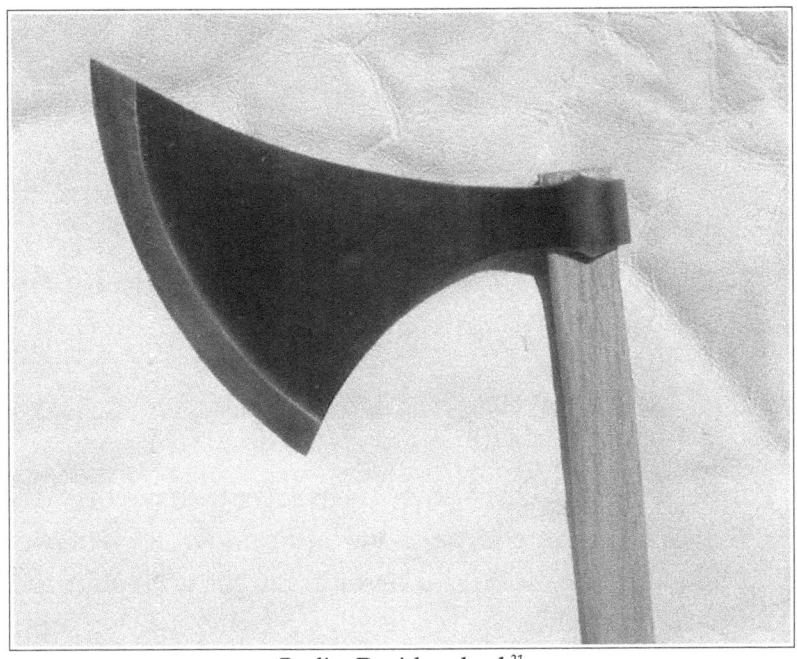

Replica Danish ax head.[21]

The cutting surface of the battle ax varied between 20 centimeters to 30 centimeters (8 to 12 inches) and the average weight was around one kilogram to two kilograms (two to four pounds). It was lightweight and resembled more of a meat cleaver than a wood ax that had devastating cutting ability.

The half (handle) of the ax ranged from 0.9 meters to 1.2 meters (3 to 4 feet) long. This enabled a powerful and controlled swing with the edge of the blade just right to cut through whatever it hits.

Dane Ax on Bayeux Tapestry.[22]

The Bayeux Tapestry shows us exactly the size of a two handed Danish Ax in comparison to the size of the wielder. The battle axes were shoulder level in length with slightly curved handles giving the blade edge a better cutting angle.

226

The Bow

The Norse used bows (Old Norse: bogi) predominately for hunting and in many cases for battle, especially in battles or attacks at sea.

Even though nautical battles were not common to the Norse whom preferred to fight on land, bows were indeed used in sea battles. They could use their bows to fire at an enemy awaiting them on the beach as they tried to land. They used the bow to attack other ships by firing arrows and throwing other missiles from their ship at the enemy's ship as they tried to clear the decks of men so the ship could be taken.

Ólaf's Saga describes the bow being used in a fight at sea in the Battle of Svölðr in 1000 AD. Einarr Þambarskelfir, an archer of King Ólaf, shot an arrow at Jarl Eirik whom was in an opposing ship and hit the tiller above his head so hard that it penetrated the wood through to the arrow's shaft.

Another shot followed with an arrow that penetrated all the way through his stool with the barbs coming out of the other side. The Jarl then ordered a man on his ship named Fin to fire back at the 'tall man by the mast,' whereas he did and hit Einarr Þambarskelfir's bow and broke it in two.

It is said that King Ólaf's ship was eventually overtaken and that King Ólaf of Norway, rather than die in the hands of his enemy, jumped over the side of the ship in full armor and drown.

One of the land battle tactics commonly employed by the Norse was to hurl and fire various missile weapons at the enemy line prior to charging. After of course, throwing a single spear over the enemy line in the name of Odin first. Gaining favor of the gods was an important ritual of battle to the Norse.

Vikings often used bows to effectively fire arrow volleys at their enemy. At short ranges it is said that a Norse arrow could pierce mail armor, but at longer ranges they only threatened the warriors not wearing armor. But fighting the enemy at a safe distance wasn't a concern to the Norse, whom would much rather get within melee range.

The Norse used short bows that were made of yew, elm, or ash and varied in size from around 1 meter to about 2 meters long. Some late examples have been found of Norse composite bows that had been strengthened with either horn or iron. At Hedeby, an important Viking trading settlement that flourished from the 8th to 11th centuries, a complete bow measuring 1.92 meters long made of yew was found. It is estimated that this war bow had a draw weight of well over 100 lbs. Most replica bows of this period have a draw weight of 100 to 130 lbs.

On average, Norse bows were able to shoot an arrow up to 200 meters. The distance an arrow traveled in a single bowshot was a commonly used unit of measurement in Viking Age Iceland. For example, in the medieval Icelandic law book, Grágás, it was required that when the court confiscated an outlaw's property, that it be within an ördrag (the distance of an arrow in a single bowshot) of the outlaw's home. The Grágás later defines an "ördrag" to be 200 "faðmar" (approximately 480 meters or about 1575 feet).

Norse arrowheads were usually of iron and made in a variety of shapes and sizes as well. Many arrowheads have been found at several Viking Age Icelandic house sites that varied in design and size, even a forked arrowhead that was probably used for bow fishing. The average lengths of Norse arrowheads ranged from 10 to 15 centimeters (4-6 inches).

Most arrowheads had a tang that allowed it to be driven into a hole of a hardwood shaft and then secured in place with cord and pitch. It is estimated that the arrow shafts were probably 70 to 80 centimeters (28 to 32 inches) long and about 10 millimeters (3/8 inch) in diameter.

Njáls Saga tells of the use of a bow by the Icelandic hero, Gunnar Hámundarson that single-handedly defended his home against an attack led by Gizurr hvíti. The hero Gunnar used his bow from a loft in the upper level of the house, to kill and wound ten of his opponents before his bow string was cut by one of the attackers. It is said that he asked his wife Hallgerður for a lock of her hair to mend the bow, but Gunnar had slapped her previously so she vindictively refused. He was then forced to fight his attackers off in hand to hand combat where he was killed.

The Spear

The spear was the favored weapon of the Norse all-father and god of war, Odin. Odin had a spear that was made from the World tree Yggdrasil named Gungnir. The Prose Edda says that Odin will carry his spear Gungnir and lead the bravest that had fallen on the battlefield and had been taken to the Halls of Valhalla. These fallen warriors from Valhalla are called the Einherjar and Odin will lead them to the battlefield during the Ragnarok event.

The spear held great symbolic importance to the Norse warrior and was the most common weapon during the early Viking Age. Spears were also cheap and easy to produce because they could be made with inferior steel. Notwithstanding, they were a very effective weapon that required minimal skill or training to use.

Most Viking spearheads were long and thin and ranged from 30 to 50 centimeters (12 to 20 inches) long. The Norse used a length of a bladed spearhead that is generally reserved in modern times for boar hunting.

Although many spears would be thrown into enemy lines, they were just as useful when employed as thrusting or slashing weapons. The length of the spear shafts averaged from 2 to 2.5 meters (6 ½ to 8 feet) long and were usually made of strong durable ash. A typical Norse spear was a long bladed spearhead mounted on a sturdy shaft.

Spearheads with wings are called krókspjót (hooked spears) in the sagas. Some larger spearheads that could be used for cutting were called höggspjót (hewing spear).

The Norse used a variety of spear types for varied kinds of combat fighting methods.

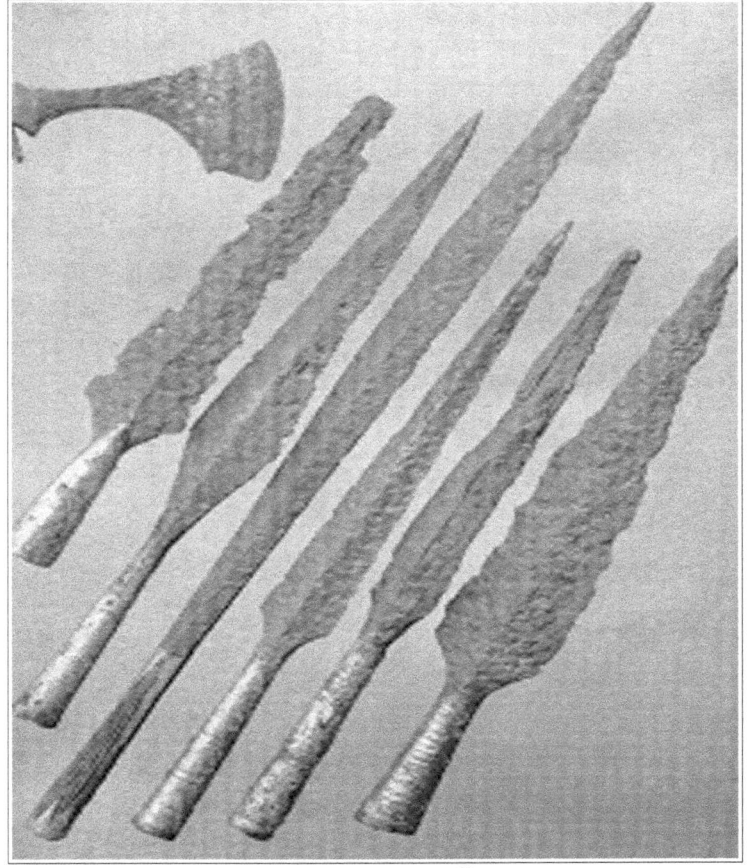

Viking Spearheads.[23]

It is likely that such spears were used in two hands. Although it has been suggested that these could be used in conjunction with a shield, it is perhaps more likely that they were used without a shield once the combat closed beyond the area in which missiles could be useful.

Lighter weight, shorter spears with narrower spearheads were used as javelins in the opening rounds of a battle. Some of these throwing spears were barbed as well. The smaller throwing spears have been found in large numbers by archeologists as the Vikings would hurl a salvo of missiles at their enemy as the lines closed.

The Viking Sagas tell of many heroes removing the pin that held the spearhead in place before throwing it, so the enemy couldn't reuse the weapon. These smaller spears could have also be used as a single-handed weapon with a shield. While the longer spears with the broader spearhead were probably used with two hands.

The Atgeir

The Atgeir was a 'spear-like spear' that was used before and through the Viking Age. One reference to the atgeir comes from Icelandic Sagas about the Viking hero Gunnar Hámundarson whom used an atgeir in Njál's Saga that would "sing" by making a ringing sound when it anticipated 'bloodshed' when it was used in battle.

The atgeir, sometimes referred to as a "mail-piercer" or "hewing-spear," was a type of polearm used throughout Scandinavia and Norse occupied areas during the Viking Age.

232

Gunnar Hámundarson fights his ambushers at Rangá.[24]

In English it is described as a kind of "halberd," but it more likely resembled a bill or glaive. The word 'atgeir' is often used to describe some typical European halberds. Additionally, some multipurpose spearheaded staves of the time period are called atgeirsstafir.

Beyond description from old records and sagas, there have not been any atgeirs discovered by archeologists to get a clear picture as to what one was beyond the assumption of it being a spearheaded type of polearm.

The Sword

A good sword was the obvious weapon of choice by the Viking Age warrior whom could afford one. Swords were found throughout Europe and it was common for a sword blade to be imported from a Frankish workshop with the hilt fittings made locally.

The most coveted of all Viking swords was a sword with the letters ULFBERHT inlaid into its blade. These very well made, high quality blades were often called an Ulfberht sword. The secrets behind the making of this special sword had long been lost for a 1000 years and they were only produced from around 800 AD to 1000 AD. The Ulfberht sword was made of the best craftsmanship and had a sharpness and strength that was unmatched. It literally was the best sword ever made in Europe and it was a Viking sword.

The typical viking sword of the day had impurities, such as slag which made it weaker including the fact that it was forged with low carbon. This made the sword soft and brittle. The steel was of poor quality and would break in battle. The typical early blacksmith of the day didn't make slag free steel. They couldn't get their fires hot enough to over 3000°f which separates the slag and allows more carbon to mix in evenly.

However, the Ulfberht sword had three times the carbon content of other medieval swords and were relatively clear of slag, making them what's called crucible steel. Crucible steel required very high heat temperatures that nobody in Europe knew how to do at the time. The method behind forging the Ulfberht sword was a closely guarded secret.

There is no archeological evidence anywhere in Europe that shows that this type of steel production was carried out. However, the Norse, especially in the Viking Age had a trade reach like no other culture and it is assumed that this steel was traded for from the Far East, possibly in Central Asia.

There have been Buddhas and rings with the name Allah inscribed on them found in Viking digs. So we know that the Norse had established trade in the Far East along the Volga Trade Route due to these objects being in Scandinavia during this time period. Some believe the steel may have originated from Iran and was traded and brought back to Norse blacksmiths whom made the sword under secret conditions.

The word Ufberht actually had two crosses in it, one before the word and one at the ending before the "t." Whereas it actually spelled "+-U-F-B-E-R-H-+-T." Archeologists have not been able to determine the meaning behind the word, *Ufberht*. It is unknown if it was the name of the designer or meant something entirely different.

Remains of an +Ulfberh+t sword in Denmark.[25]

Getting your hands on a real Ulfberht sword was difficult and extremely expensive and there were many counterfeits.   Most swords of the time were made from low carbon steel by means of pattern welding. A method where the central section of the blade was made from twisted rods of iron and pounded together forming a strong and pliable core, then a harder (but more brittle) edge was then welded to the core.

Example of pattern forged sword.[26]

When the quality and knowledge of iron smelting improved, in addition to purer and more regular sources of iron becoming more readily available, the method of pattern welding was discontinued.

Viking Armor

The Norse warrior often wore chain mail armor whenever he could get his hands upon a set. Although chain mail wasn't as common as one may think. This was due to the amount of iron needed and the time it took to make the armor in the first place. This made chain mail expensive and was generally only wore by those whom could afford it.

Chain mail grew more available when iron became more readily available and smelting techniques significantly improved. It would still take many hours upon hours of chain mail pattern linking to make a complete chain mail shirt.

The speed of chain mail manufacturing improved with the wealth of the blacksmith, as he'd have plentiful access to iron and many skilled thralls tasked to linking the mail. A task that was tedious at every step, as rod had to be first made from iron scraps. Then countless numbers of chain links cut from the rod to be shaped into rings and then 'knitted' in a precised pattern to create the unique and superior chain mail only the Norse made.

There's a fragmented, yet mostly complete example of a Norse chain mail tunic that's been found at the Gjermundbu burial site. Although many partial examples of chain mail exist and there are several historical recordings of Norse use of chain mail; The chain mail found at the Gjermundbu site is the only nearly complete set that's ever found.

Brynja or coat of chain mail, found in Thorsberg moor, Germany.[27]

The Norse mentioned chain mail in their Sagas which they called, 'byrnie' or 'brynja.' These were long tunics of chain mail armor that reached below the waist to protect the wearer from sword cuts.

238

Of course chain mail armor alone wasn't enough protection. It was essential to wear thick padding underneath the mail to absorb the force of a sword or ax blow. You also needed protection from spear and arrow strikes.

Reindeer hide is said to have been worn by the Norse underneath chain mail and was used alone as armor as well. Reindeer hide was reputedly said to be more effective even than chain mail. Quite often, reindeer hide would've been worn under chain mail for padding and to serve as additional protection. More correctly though, the Norse warrior would have wore reindeer hide armor with chain mail over it as additional protection.

Some examples of viking era chain mail are made up of interlocking rings that were riveted together. But the better chain mail shirts were of alternating slag rings and riveted rings. This made the chain mail armor stronger. A tribute to Norse ingenuity.

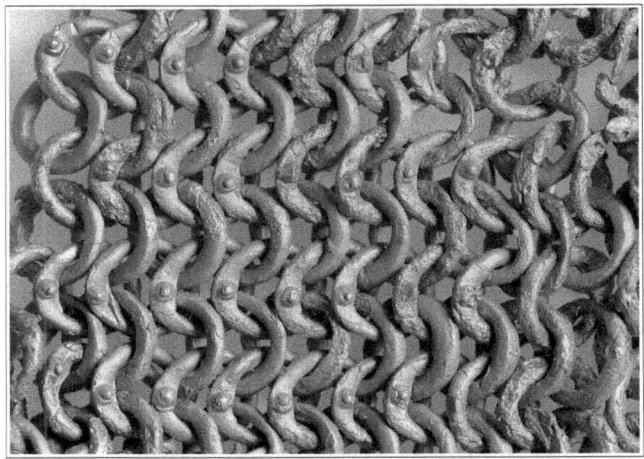

Chainmail sample found in Gjermundbu, Norway.[28]

Scale armor or lamellar armor was occasionally obtained from the East and had been replicated by Norse armorers by using either leather or metal scales. Pieces of scale or lamellar armor have been found at Norse burial sites in: Birka, Sweden, Kertch (Crimea), Ukraine (dated 5th century), and Krefeld-Gellup, Germany (dated 6th century) and Niederstotzingen, Germany (dated 7th century).

Viking warrior in replica lamellar armor, spangenhelm with attached chainmail.[29]

The lamellar armor found at the burial ground from Krefeld Gellep was at least a two-piece set and resembles the lamellar armor found at Niederstotzingen, Germany. A leather or reindeer coat was probably worn underneath the armor to absorb the blows.

Viking Helms

Contrary to the popular belief that Vikings wore horned helmets, there is no evidence that this ever happened. The horned and winged helmets were an invention of 19th century art and theater. If you think about it, as cool as a horned helm looks would be extremely impractical. It would not deflect blows, but rather 'catch' them. The horns would catch everything a wearer walked past. Wearing a horned or winged helmet would be a nightmare.

The real Norse / Viking helm was usually made from four plates of iron in the shape of a rounded cap in the **spangenhelm** pattern with an iron "spectacle" visor that formed around the eyes and over the nose.

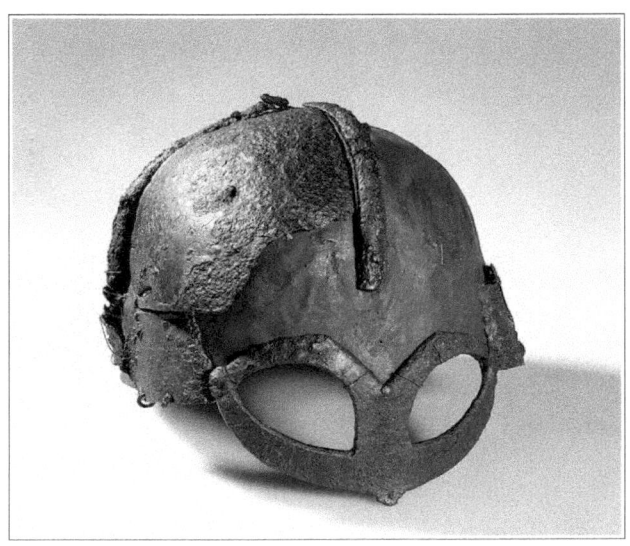

From a 10th century Norway chieftain's grave, the only known complete helm.[30]

Some Helms were made of a simpler pattern with a peaked top and had just a piece of iron as a nose guard, instead of a full visor. This style of helmet was more practical and functional. The Norse helm had a peak and was smooth, this would deflect a blow much better. The nose guard protected the face. A helm wasn't worn by itself but you generally had padding to absorb blows and a chain mail coif to protect the neck and sides of the face from slashes.

Some spangenhelms had a chain mail coif attached to the sides of the helm that would drop down to protect the wearer's neck. This was for those not wearing a full chain mail coif underneath the helmet. This was in addition to a thick cap worn under the helm for padding to absorb the shock of any blows to the head.

Replica Spangenhelm with nose guard .[31]

Chapter 13 – Norse Longships

The Norse longship is perhaps one of the most recognizable cultural icons of the Vikings. No one else had ships like these and these ships were ahead of their time. The Longships were deeply rooted in Norse culture and their way of life. They were a necessity that enabled the Norse to not only survive, but thrive in their tough terrain.

Much of Scandinavia was of mountainous terrain with fjords and inlets everywhere along its coastlines. This is where the majority of the Norse lived, along the rugged coastline. Inland trade was difficult, cumbersome, and outright dangerous. Movement by ship was really the only feasible way. This led to the incredible high degree of technology and innovation that the Norse put behind designing their ships.

The hjortspring boats from the Norse Pre-Roman Iron Age were designed as a large canoe which evolved from the Umiak type of canoe that was also used by the Inuit (Eskimo) people. The early Norse used this type of boat very similarly as did the Inuits in a sense of hunting and "getting around" locally.

Norse boats were later built in a way where the edges of the hull planks overlapped in a construction method known in shipbuilding as the "clinker" method.

The planks were joined end to end into a 'strake,' which is part of the shell of the hull that runs longitudinally along the ship's sides. This technique was developed in Northern Europe and the Norse used it very successfully.

Longship displaying the 'clinker' construction method of overlapping planks.[32]

It has also been found that the clinker built planks helped hydroplane the ship as it moved and literally glided it across the water. This design made Norse ships faster.

246

The longship was a design that evolved from the umiak canoe design from the Stone Ages to the graceful longships used during the Viking era. The longships were very lightweight, sleek and graceful. They were designed to have a narrow hull which made them not only faster, but they were able to navigate shallow rivers and even permitted beach landings.

The longships were also double ended like a canoe, which allowed it to reverse direction without turning the boat around. The ship's high maneuverability was a useful trait to have in the northern waters where sea ice and icebergs were present. The longship was fitted with oars all along its sides and the later models were also fitted with a large rectangular sail. Norse sails were made from rough wool cloth that were hung on a single mast that would replace the rowers or supplement them. The typical speed of the Longships was around 5 to 10 knots, with a top speed of 15 knots under favorable conditions. A speed on water that was lightning fast in comparison to any other seaworthy vessel of the day.

Longships were highly prized items that were usually owned by farmers and fishermen and then were commissioned by Kings and Jarls for use in warfare during times of conflict or for use in viking raids. The longships were not warships, but would be used as troop transports to carry men.

In that very rare instance that longships were ever used in battle on water, the ships would be tied together to create a steady platform for infantry to fight and archers to fire missiles from. Javelins and spears would be thrown too.

The Longships evolved into such seaworthiness that they were able to be used to navigate across the ocean. The longship has even reached Greenland and the New World, a place which the Norse called Vinland.

This was not only an attribution to the Norse Longship, but to Norse navigation that allowed them to reach such great distances at will.

Navigation at sea, particularly in the North sea where fog and overcast skies that last days long can hide the Sun. This makes finding the direction one is traveling to be an undertaking that would seem nearly impossible. Nothing is worse than being completely lost at sea. However, the Norse were able to overcome this obstacle with an object called a **sunstone**. The sunstone was a transparent crystal that refracted the Sun's light and revealed its position.

Iceland spar, perhaps the medieval sunstone.[33]

This once seemingly mythical object has been found in ship wreckage and has revealed itself to be a real object. The object had been spoken about being used to help Norse seamen navigate the Northern seas which can at times be impossible to navigate by using the sun or stars. Especially when you cannot see the sun or stars and have no idea which way you're going.

Previously, such a glass or crystal that could be used to find the sun in dense fog had never been found. It was assumed that its existence was a myth, such as sea monsters the Norse wrote about. But one has been found in a wreckage and it actually works!

The sunstone was a crystal called an Icelandic Spar or Calcite Crystal. What this object did was refract the light and reveal the Sun's position, in fog, haze, overcast and even after the Sun had just dipped below the horizon. This was the navigational device that allowed such far reaching seafaring conducted by the Vikings.

Chapter 14 - The Skræling

When the Vikings reached the New World, they called the native inhabitants (American Indians or Native Americans), "**Skræling**." There has been much debate as to what exactly this word or label meant. Some translate it as "skin wearers," which may be true as to how they described them. The Norse generally wore woolen or linen clothing and North American Natives generally wore animal skins.

There was one thing that is puzzling about the Norse describing their interactions or meeting the Skræling. The Viking explorers weren't curious or baffled by these new people. They acted as if they'd come into contact with people like this before and their way of life. This is significant because it tells us that the Skræling were a fairly or at not unusual sighting by the Norse.

For example, 500 years later when other Europeans had come to the New World (The Americas), they were ultimately curious of these strange new people they had never seen before. They were curious of their ways and everything about them. But not the Norse, they didn't appear to be curious at all and merely noted interacting with these people. The Norse reaction seems to hint that they'd come into contact with people like this on a fairly regular basis.

This is because the Norse did in fact have regular contact and knowledge of these people. The Skræling and Thule people were commonly referred to by the Norse. The island of Thule, which is now called Qaanaaq, is located in northwest Greenland towards Canada and is part of the Kingdom of Denmark. It is believed the Thule people are the ancestors of the modern Inuit (Eskimo) as they are linked biologically, culturally, and linguistically.

The Vikings were in regular contact with the Thule people, particularly in the 11th century when they explored Greenland and the edges of Canada where they referred to these people as both "Thule" and "Skræling." During the occurrence of the "Little Ice Age" from 1650 AD to 1850 AD, the climate changed and caused the Thule communities to migrate. These people scattered and resettled in different areas. They later became known as the Eskimo and then later became known as the Inuit People.

Another very significant group of people that the Norse were in continual contact with were the Sami people (Sámi or Saami). The Sami are an indigenous Finno-Ugric people who inhabit the Arctic area of what's called "Sápmi" today.

The area of Sápmi encompasses much of the northern halves of Norway and Sweden along with the far northern portion of Finland including the Kola Peninsula of Russia.

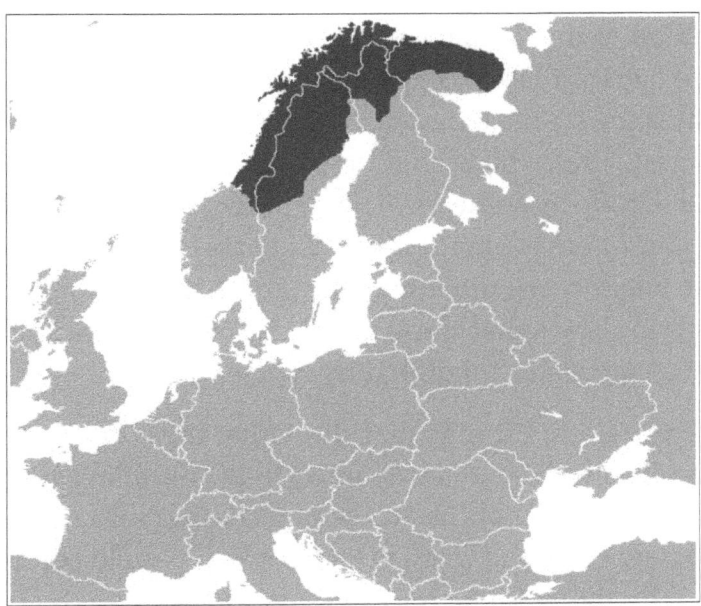

Map of the Saami Homeland by Rogper, 4 May 2004.

The Sami languages are a part of the Uralic language family, a language family that is associated with native speakers of Estonian, Finnish, and Hungarian. Language regions today that are also traditionally known to be areas that were either part of or in contact with the Norse.

The first mention of a Uralic people was in Tacitus's Germania, mentioning the Fenni (usually interpreted as referring to the Sami) and two other possibly Uralic tribes living in the farthest reaches of Scandinavia.

In recent times, linguists often place the Urheimat (*Urheimat is a term that refers to the original homeland of the language*) of the Proto-Uralic language in the vicinity of the Volga River, west of the Urals, close to the Urheimat of the Indo-European languages, or to the east and southeast of the Urals.

Related to this Uralic language is the language of the North American Eskimo. The Eskimo–Uralic hypothesis associates the Uralic languages with the Eskimo–Aleut languages. Uralo-Siberian is an expanded form of the Eskimo–Uralic hypothesis. The hypothesis associates the Uralic languages with Yukaghir, Chukotko-Kamchatkan, and the Eskimo–Aleut languages. This linguistic connection shows that these people were in or near the areas that were also inhabited by Norse people.

There are other things that show that the Norse were very familiar with and accustomed to the Skræling people. It's very probable that the Norsemen coming into contact, either knew of or had dealt with Skræling people before. This is why they didn't concern themselves too much with meeting 'Native Americans' as did the latter explorers in the late 15th and early 16th centuries when they began coming to the New World and meeting the Native Americans.

The Norse were already very acquainted with a people they called Skræling. A more primitive people that Norse explorers and traders would occasionally come into contact with. The Norse also had contact with the Sami people that were located just North of them. These were a people the Norse had regular contact and interactions with due to proximity to each other. Contact between cultures which exists Today by modern Scandinavians.

This contact of Northern people was extended with the Thule people (Eskimos / Inuits) across the North where the Norse traveled all the way to the New World. A land which the Norse referred to as Vinland.

There were many commonalities of these people, such as how the Nordic Sami and the Skræling lived. Look below at the comparisons of Sami lavvo tents in North Scandinavia to that of the Native American (Skræling) teepees most commonly knows from the North American Great Plains.

A Sami indigenous northern European family in Norway around 1900.[34]

The above picture is of the Sami people in Norway and the picture taken below is of the Sami people in Lapland. Both in Northern parts of Scandinavia.

Nordic Sami (Saami) people in Sapmi (Lapland) in front of two Lavvo Tents.[35]

The following pictures are of teepees made by the Great Plains Natives (Indians) in North America. Note how they are almost identical to the tents made by the Sami.

A young Oglala girl sitting in front of a tipi, 1891.[36]

The above photograph and watercolor painting on the next page are both of Native American shelters in the North American Great Plains. The style of housing between the two cultures is astoundingly almost identical.

Sioux Teepees. 1832-1834.[37]

Not only did the Norse tell of the Skræling people that they encountered over the centuries, but the aboriginals also tell of making contact with the Norse. The Inuit (Eskimos) have a tale about a Kavdlunait (Inuit word for foreigner or European) that was speared by a Kayaker and how they feared revenge from the Kavdlunait because of the killing.

Violence was the usual interaction between the two people, inhibiting peaceful trade and any real successful settling of these areas by Viking explorers. Such stories are also mentioned in the Saga of Erik the Red and the Greenlander Saga written in the 13th century, about Thorvald and Thorfinn Karlsefni's attempt to settle in Vinland.

Thorvald's first contact with the native inhabitants, whom would come to be known as the Skrælings. he'd captured and killed eight of the inhabitants when they were attacked at their beached ships. Thorvald is said to have been wounded by an arrow that flew between the edge of the ship and a shield, lodging into his armpit which had been the cause of his death.

Thorfinn, after barely surviving a rugged winter, had at first made peaceful interacts and trade with the Skræling they'd came into contact with. Only later did the peaceful interactions end when Thorfinn's men came under attack after a native had been frightened by a bull that had gotten loose. The settlement was forced to retreat to more defensible ground and fight back where it was reported that he had lost two men and the Skræling had lost several of theirs.

The Norse explorers pointed out that despite all that the land offered in these areas, they would be under constant attack by Skræling. At this point, the Norse and Skræling were already at war with one another and any further peaceful contact between the two people was simply not going to happen.

There have been recent findings in DNA research where they analyze a type of DNA that is passed only from mother to child. Using this research, scientists have found more than 80 living Icelanders with a genetic variation similar to one found mostly in Native Americans.

This signature DNA probably entered Icelandic bloodlines around the time period of 1000 AD when the first Viking-American Indian child was probably born. It is believed that a Native American female was transported from Vinland to Iceland on one of the Viking voyages, as the Norse were well known to capture inhabitants on their raids.

The North Americans and the North Europeans had known and had contact with each other for a very long time.

Additionally, new archaeological data and the latest DNA research have revealed that Europeans had indeed visited North American shores far earlier than the Vikings. These findings date arrivals to approximately 17,000 years before Columbus was even born. This was a time when the two regions were connected by land-ice bridges and from hunters following seals along the ice's edge.

This explains why the North American natives and the Norse Viking explorers were of no surprise to each other when the Norse explorers spoke of them. They had been in previous contact off and on with each other for not hundreds, but thousands of years.

Chapter 15 - The Jötnar (Giants)

The jötnar pronounced "yoot-nar" (singular: jotunn or jotun) also known as the þursar (singular þurs, pronounced "thurs") are a race of giants that live in Jötunheimr. Jötunheimr literally translates from Old Norse as "Giant Home." There was also referencing to Utgard (Old Norse Útgarðr) in Norse Mythology as being the home of giants.

Jötunheimr or rather Jotunheim was a place high in the mountains where men could not go. There is an actual reference to this location in Southern Norway called the Jotunheimen Mountains which is part of the Scandinavian Mountains. The high mountains of Jotunheim is where the Norse believed the majority of giants lived.

In Norse mythology and in the Sagas, the Norse spoke quite frequently about the presence or rather nuisance of giants. Mostly there is mention of the frost giants, but there were many other types of giants and they came with a variety of names and descriptions that went from trolls, to ogres, to many other large humanoid beings.

The Norse were very animate about the fact there were indeed giants, sharing the Earth with them. So much so, that they mentioned some of the gods, kings, and a few heroes even marrying them and producing human/giant hybrids as offspring. The Norse also mentioned that it was for the better of mankind to slay the giants and try to rid them from the World. From about every Norse account, there was always conflict and competition between giants and mankind.

This brings us to an interesting theory. Perhaps there is some truth to the presence of giants at one time in our history. We all know that myths tend to have some truth mixed in with them. Quite often myths are made up to explain unknown things at the time and are often quite hard for the modern thinker to believe. Myths come from oral histories, beliefs, and traditions that are passed on generation to generation. As highlighted at the beginning of this book, the history of the Norse did not begin over a millennium ago during the "Viking Age." Their history began much earlier and roots their very beginnings before the Stone age. With that being said, you must consider that these myths were created and passed down many generations as with other knowledge and skills such as hunting, fishing, etc..

Now, we know that different early races of man inhabited the European regions at the same time and one of the questions that has formed in the minds of modern man Today is: what happened to the Neanderthal man?

If you haven't already figured out where I may be going with this, I will lay it out. I understand that this theory may appear to be a bit far fetched, but be rest assured that it will make perfect sense.

What if the homo sapiens (humans) that were in the area, whom we later call *the Norse* were in contact with the Neanderthals. It is not unheard of, in fact we've found evidence that shows that the two races knew of each other.

But what we don't know is what happened to the Neanderthal. Did they simply die out in Natural Selection as the World changed after the Ice age and were not able to make the necessary changes in diet and habit needed to adapt and survive. Or were they simply killed off by the Homo Sapiens (humans) that came to the area. The later argument is strong as the conflict for food, hunting areas, and simply encroaching on each other's territories would have caused a struggle where the homo sapiens prevailed. There is also a third theory that goes along with the killing off the Neanderthal is that they were also mated out of existence.

The Neanderthal genome project confirmed this while examining mitochondrial DNA comparing Neanderthals and modern humans. The project discovered that there is a percentage of about 1 - 4% of Neanderthal DNA that make up part of genetic contribution of non-African modern humans. This means that there is about 1% to 4% Neanderthal DNA in non-African modern humans living today.

We quite possibly killed and bred the Neanderthal out of existence. This also highlights some of the Old Norse Myths and religion that claim the Norse gods (often Norse kings or heroes) had married and bred with the 'giants.'

This may also explain why so many Scandinavians are so tall - although a bit far fetched. In the myths it is said that the gods bred with the giants and created hybrid mixes. Then later, killed most of the jötnar off as enemies to mankind. This makes sense as to what happened to the jötnar (Giants, Trolls, Ogres and other names they were referred to). By description of these beings from myth and tales, it also leads to great possibility that the jötnar were none other than the Neanderthals.

This theory can even be expanded that the Neanderthal we not only the giants (jötnar) that the Norse referred to, but Neanderthals or similar, such as the Denisova hominins recently discovered in Siberia, could be what the Native Americans referred to as Sasquatch (Big Foot) and Asians as Yeti.

Of course, these are only theories. But it is quite probable that the Neanderthals were in fact the Giants known to the Norse that eventually disappeared or died out.

References

1   Kouwenhoven, Arlette P. "World's Oldest Spears." Archaeological Institute of America. Volume 50 Number 3, May/June 1997.
2   A drawing of a point from the paleolithic Hamburg culture arrow head. Drawing by Micke. 2007.
3   Drawing of a Ahrensburg point, Germany. José-Manuel Benito. August 2006.
4   Linear Band Pottery, Collection University of Jena, Bereich für Ur- und Frühgeschichte an der Friedrich-Schiller-Universität Jena. Photo by Roman Grabolle. January 2005.
5   Map of European Middle Neolithic Period. Created by Joostik. December 2012.
6   Tunnackigyxa (thin-neck axe), from Skåne. 1st (1876–1899), 2nd (1904–1926) or 3rd (1923–1937) edition of Nordisk familjebok.
7   Boat-shaped battle axes typical of the Battle Axe Culture. Pottery vessels and axes, chisels and arrows made of flint were also common. The National Museum of Denmark. 2013.
8   Corded ware pottery from around 2500 BC in the Museum für Vor- und Frühgeschichte (Museum of prehistory and early history), Berlin. Photo by Einsamer Schütze. June 2011.
9   Two of the viking stone ships (burial grounds) at Badelunda near Västerås, Sweden. Photo by: "Berig." 1 May 2005.
10 A modern version of England 878 AD made using Inkscape by Hel-hama. 13 June 2012.
11 The approximate extent of Old Norse and related languages in the early 10th century. Created by Wiglaf, based on Europe plain rivers by Dbachmann. 20 April 2005.
12 Gwyn Jones. A History of the Vikings. Oxford: Oxford University Press. 1968. p. 177.
13 Ian Riddler. Two Late Saxon Combs from the Longmarket Excavations. Canterbury's Archaeology 1989/1990, The 14th Annual Report of Canterbury Archaeological Trust Ltd.
14 Reconstruction of the Køstrup apron-dress at the National Museum of Denmark. Photo by Hilde Thunem
15 Wikinger Museum Foteviken auf Skanör. Wikinger (Guide in Wikingerkleidung) Wolfgang Sauber. 17 August 2007.
16 Germanic thing, drawn after the depiction in a relief of the Column of Marcus Aurelius (AD 193)
17 Egill Skallagrímsson engaging in holmgang with Berg-Önundr, painting by Johannes Flintoe (1787–1870)
18 Fig. 885. Drawing of a Shield from Gokstad ship. CH 6, pg 98. "The Viking Age" vol. 1 by Paul B Du Chaillu. 1889.

19 Modern reconstructions of Viking shield. Danish National Museum. Photo: Jacob Nyborg Andreassen. Accessed online 2013.

20 Viking "bearded axe" blade 1000 AD (top), and a German horseman's axe blade 1100 AD (bottom). Incitatus. 4 December 2006.

21 Replica Danish ax head. Forged by Bronze Lion. 14 August 2008.

22 Infantry armed with spears, swords and battle axes that fought the huscarls Harold Hastings. Bayeux Tapestry, Bayeux. Picture by Urban, February 2005.

23 Viking Spearheads. The Vikings (Pelican Books ISBN 10: 0140204598 / ISBN 13: 9780140204599) by Brondsted, Johannes. 1960.

24 From Njáls saga: Gunnar fights his ambushers at Rangá. Illustration from "Vore fædres liv" : karakterer og skildringer fra sagatiden / samlet og udggivet af Nordahl Rolfsen ; oversættelsen ved Gerhard Gran., Kristiania: Stenersen, 1898.

25 Ulfberth sword found in Finland at the National Museum in Copenhagen, Denmark (Historisk Viden, Danmark). 2013 online.

26 Example of pattern forged sword at the National Museum in Copenhagen, Denmark (Historisk Viden, Danmark). 2013 online.

27 Thorsberg moor, Germany find. Fig. 412. Brynja or coat of chain mail, 3 feet long. CH 12. pg 215. "The Viking Age" vol 2 by Paul B Du Chaillu. 1889.

28 Chainmail sample from the mail shirt found in Gjermundbu, Norway. Universitets Oldsaksamling in Oslo, Norway. Accessed 2013.

29 Viking warrior with leather lamellar armour. Via Elettra Gardini www.pinterest.com 2013. Note: the original source of this picture is of yet to be found. It was used in 'fair use' as the best example of replicated lamellar armor in use to educate the reader in their research on Viking armor.

30 Viking helmet from the Gjermundbu gravesite now in the Museum of Cultural History, University of Oslo. Photo: NTNU Museum February 10, 2010.

31 Replica Conical Spangenhelm with nasal made from 16 gauge steel by Royal Oak Armoury Artisan Crafts / Metal Work. Photo taken by Royal Oak Armoury on June 15, 2012.

32 Gokstadskipet, Vikingskipmuseet, Oslo. Photo by Karamell 2005.

33 Iceland spar, perhaps the medieval sunstone. Decemeber 2010 by ArniEin.

34 A Sami indigenous northern European family in Norway around 1900. The picture was probably taken in 1896 by an unknown author.

35 Nordic Sami (Saami) people in Sapmi (Lapland) in front of two Lavvo Tents. Photo taken 1900-1920 by Granbergs Nya Aktiebolag.

36 A young Oglala girl sitting in front of a tipi, with a puppy beside her,

probably on or near Pine Ridge Reservation. Photo taken 1891 by John C. H. Grabill.

37 Sioux Teepees. Watercolor on paper by Karl Bodmer from his travel to the U.S. 1832-1834.

Cover art made from original painting: The Ravager (1909) by artist John Charles Dollman (1851-1934).

38. Christian Krohg: Illustration for Olav Tryggvasons saga, Heimskringla 1899.

39. Hamilton, Hugo. 1830. Sketches of Scandinavia's ancient history. Stockholm: Gjöthström & Magnusson.

40. "The destruction of Irminsul by Charlemagne" (1882) by Heinrich Leutemann. - Wägner, William. 1882. Nordic-Germanic gods and heroes. Otto Spamer, Leipzig and Berlin. Page 159.

41. Lindisfarne Priory Viking stone, a 9th Century grave marker with seven warriors carved into the surface. Holy Island, Northumberland.

42. Statue of a Viking in Gimli, Manitoba (Canada). Photo by Magickallwiz, 2008.

43. Lindisfarne shown within Northumberland. Northumberland UK location map by Nilfanion, 2010.

44. One of three wooden spears found at Schöningen, Germany. Photo by: Chip Clark, Smithsonian Institution. 1995.

45. John Cassell. 19th century depiction of a Pict. *John Cassell's Illustrated History of England: volume 1 From the earliest period to the reign of Edward the Fourth.* Cassell, Petter & Galpin. 1865.

46. The Danish Ship called the Raven, Viking Ship, Pre-800 AD. Historical archives of LIFE Magazine.

47. "King Rorik" by Hermanus Willem Koekkoek (1867–1929) *Teutonic Myth and Legend* by Donald A. MacKenzie, London, Gresham Publications. 1912.

48. *King Ælla of Northumbria's execution of Ragnar Lodbrok.* Hamilton, Hugo. 1830. Teckningar ur Skandinaviens Äldre Historia. Stockholm: Gjöthström & Magnusson.

49. Peter Nicolai Arbo. *Battle of Stamford Bridge.* December 31, 1869.

50. A battle between 'Anglo-Saxons' and 'Vikings'. Staged by 're-enactors.' Source: bbc.co.uk.

51. King of Mercia Athelred seen on the exterior of Lichfield Cathedral.

52. Reenactors depicting King Alfred with the West Saxon (Wessox) forces battling the Danish Norsemen of the Great Summer Army.

53. Statue of King Alfred at Wantage created by DJ Clayworth. 2004.

54. Statue of the first King of Norway, Harald Hårfagre (Fairhair). Made by Einar Jónsson in 1924 and located on Arnarhóll, Reykjavík.

55. *Viking Ships besieging Paris*. Der Spiegel Geschichte (6/2010): The Vikings - Warriors culture: The life of the Northmen. Spiegel-Verlag Rudolf Augstein GmbH & Co. KG, Hamburg 2010, p.33
56. Portrait of Charles the Bald (823-877) at Palace of Versailles, France.
57. A map of the routes taken by the Great Heathen Army from 865 to 878 based on Stenton 'Anglo-Saxon England' chapter 8 and Hill ' An Atlas of Anglo-Saxon England' p40-1. by Hel-hama. June 26, 2012.
58. Map of the Duchy of Normandy.
59. Portrait of Robert I of Western Francia, King of the Franks.
60. British Isles in 10th century represented with the coastline at the time. Created by Ikonact. August 31, 2013.
61. Rollo statue depicted among the 6 dukes of Normandy in the town square of Falaise.
62. Silver penny of Eric Bloodaxe. A coin of the last Viking King of York, Northumbria. It circulated during the Viking Age at 947 to 954 AD. British Museum.
63. Raven's Banner (hrafnsmerki) as used by Jarl Sigurd.
64. Erik the Red statue at Qagssiarssuk, Greenland.
65. Leif Erikson statue in front of Hallgrimskirkja.Iceland.
66. A depiction of the death of Thorvald Eriksson which took place somewhere in North America in 1004 AD. *Did the Vikings Beat the Pilgrims to Plymouth?* By Patrick Browne. July 24, 2014
67. Death of Ymir. Lorenz Frølich (25 October 1820 – 25 October 1908).
68. Illustration of Auðumbla licking Búri out of a salty ice-block, from an Icelandic 18th century manuscript by Jakob Sigurðsson.(1765-1766).
69. Two dwarfs as depicted in the Poetic Edda poem Völuspá by Lorenz Frølich. 1895.
70. "The Wolves Pursuing Sol and Mani." J.C. Dollman. 1909.
71. Scultpure of the first living people, Ask and Embla, at the main square in Sölvesborg, Sweden.
72. Artist's depiction of Yggdrasil and the nine realms.
73. Odin the Wanderer by George von Rosen. 1896.
74. Odin sits atop his steed Sleipnir, his ravens Huginn and Muninn and wolves Geri and Freki nearby by Lorenz Frølich. 1895.
75. Odin Hanging on the World Tree. Illustration for Die Edda: Germanische Götter und Heldensagen by Hans von Wolzogen. 1920.
76. "Frigg and Odin in Grímnismál by Frølich" by Lorenz Frølich. Published in Gjellerup, Karl.1895.
77. Statute of Balder. Sculpted by Bengt Erland Fogelberg. 1842.
78. Artist depiction of Thor Odinsson with Toothgrinder and Toothgnasher. mytholipedia.com. 2014.

79. Drawing of silver amulet representing Mjöllnir, the hammer of Thor. Discovered in Skåne, Sweden.1877.
80. Artist's depiction of the Tyr, God of War.
81. The Battle of Thor with the serpent of Midgard. Painted by Henry Fuseli. Royal Academy of Arts, London. 1788.
82. Artist's depiction of the Symbol of Jörmungandr, The Midgard Serpent.
83. "The Punishment of Loki", by Louis Huard. *The Heroes of Asgard: Tales from Scandinavian Mythology* by A & E Keary. MacMillan & Co, London. 1891.
84. The Norse god Heimdallr blowing the horn Gjallarhorn by Lorenz Frølich (1820-1908).
85. "The goddess Sif" by John Charles Dollman. *Myths of the Norsemen from the Eddas and Sagas* by Guerber, H. A.. London. 1909.
86. "Hermod before Hela" by John Charles Dollman. *Myths of the Norsemen from the Eddas and Sagas* by Guerber, H. A.. London. 1909.
87. The god Freyr by Johannes Gehrts. 1901.
88. "Kampf der untergehenden Götter" by Friedrich Wilhelm Heine.1882.
89. Njord's desire of the Sea by W. G. Collingwood. 1908.
90. Skadi's longing for the Mountains by W. G. Collingwood. 1908.
91. Týr and Fenrir by John Bauer. 1911.
92. Hel by Johannes Gehrts. 1889.
93. An illustration of Lífþrasir and Líf by Lorenz Frølich.Published in Den ældre Eddas Gudesange by Gjellerup, Karl. 1895.
94. The battle between Surtr and Freyr at Ragnarök, illustration by Lorenz Frølich. Published in Den ældre Eddas Gudesange by Gjellerup, Karl. 1895.
95. The Sutton Hoo helmet located at the British Museum. 2011.
96. Replica of Viking Era Merchant Knarr. Publishied in *Mobility, the Viking Way*. By Alan Robert Lancaster. March 28, 2015.